The Lazarus Blueprint

ANCIENT SECRETS FOR HEALING AND INNER PEACE

Mary-Alice and Richard Jafolla

Also by the Authors

The Simple Truth

The Quest

Adventures on the Quest

Quest for Prayer

Quest '96 Calendar Journal

Quest '97 Calendar Journal

Quest 2000 Calendar Journal

Nourishing the Life Force

The Lazarus Blueprint

ANCIENT SECRETS FOR HEALING AND INNER PEACE

Mary-Alice and Richard Jafolla

Unity Village, Missouri 64065-0001

The Lazarus Blueprint
A Unity Books Paperback Original

Unity Books are available at special discounts for bulk purchases for study groups, book clubs, sales promotions, book signings or fundraising. To place an order, call the Unity Customer Care Department at 1-866-236-3571 or email *wholesaleaccts@unityonline.org*.

Cover design: Hailee Pavey, Multimedia Artist, Unity
Interior design: The Covington Group, Kansas City, Missouri

Library of Congress Control Number: 2012933866

ISBN: 978-0-87159-359-7

Canada BN 13252 0933 RT

CONTENTS

The art world often uses X-rays and infrared techniques to verify a painting's authenticity. Sometimes, quite unexpectedly, they discover another painting underneath. The portrait of a woman was discovered underneath Van Gogh's *Patch of Grass*. A Leonardo da Vinci sketch was hiding behind his venerated *Virgin on the Rocks*. An earlier Picasso painting lies under his famous *Rue de Montmartre*.

In each case, a masterpiece beneath a masterpiece lay unseen and unappreciated, sometimes for centuries.

A hidden masterpiece also lies beneath the Lazarus story.

An Ancient Secret Hiding in
Plain Sight

The Lazarus Blueprint will bring to light the masterpiece that lay beneath the biblical story for 2,000 years.

This book approaches the Lazarus story from a fresh, new perspective—a nonreligious perspective. You see, woven throughout the ancient story, yet concealed in plain sight, lies an extraordinary blueprint for overcoming a difficult situation, and healing even a situation that may seem impossible.

Are you struggling with this kind of problem?

Whatever your need—physical, mental, emotional, spiritual—this valuable information hidden beneath the surface of the Lazarus story outlines Six Steps you can use to overcome an unwanted situation and redesign your life.

It doesn't matter what degree of authenticity you ascribe to the biblical story. View the original story any way you wish: religiously, intellectually, skeptically or indifferently. That's outside the scope of this book. The fundamental principles embedded in the Lazarus story reach *beyond* the story itself and will always remain the same—consistent, unchanging, powerful.

Making the "Impossible"
Possible

Something deep within the human spirit yearns to triumph, no matter how impossible a situation seems. We search for answers. Sometimes, if we can just hold on, just wait long enough, the ebb and flow of changing circumstances will carry us out of the depths of darkness back up into the sunlight. Things get better.

Sometimes they don't.

Sometimes we feel trapped in a situation we can't control and think only a miracle could move us back into the flow of life. We don't know where to turn. We don't know where to look for help. We wonder if any help even exists.

It does.

Incredible storehouses of wisdom and possibilities are available to us that, *when we open ourselves to them,* will lead to an outcome we would have believed impossible.

Help Is Available

Need help with a physical healing? Emotional healing? Trying to restore a relationship? Have an addiction problem? The steps embedded in the Lazarus story, when you apply them to your specific situation, can help lead you to the solution. Together the steps form a psychologically and spiritually sound blueprint to get you started on your own path back into the flow of life.

This blueprint is so basic, so universal, so timeless and so powerful that it can work for *everyone*. Whatever your situation, the steps outlined in the blueprint can be your guide. Clearly laid out for you to follow, the instructions show you how to turn your "impossibility" into "possibility."

"I Can Do It Too"

The Lazarus Blueprint is the culmination of a series of classes and workshops we, the authors, presented. Many who worked with the Six Steps shared their stories with us. You will read the accounts of some of these people at the end of each chapter. Their names have been changed, but their stories are genuine and heartwarming. We include them because another person's success can inspire and motivate you, and help you feel *"I can do it too!"*

Maybe you have been reading these words because you are searching for help to be free of some unwelcome condition or situation in your life. If so, you, too, can use this blueprint to overcome that "impossibility" facing you today. You can redesign your life.

Timing is everything.

Now may be the time for *you* to discover the dynamic help this blueprint offers.

Help
From the Past

Let's review the original Lazarus story. Throughout the book, we will be working with key passages, although not from the usual religious perspective. We delve into these passages because they carry the blueprint for redesigning your life and turning the impossible into the possible. Cloaked in its biblical setting, the 2,000-year-old blueprint soon proves its ability to stand alone *beyond* the biblical story as timeless, universal and decidedly current.

The Six Steps of the blueprint can help you restore your life. Hope instead of despair, light instead of darkness, and a certain knowing deep within you that things are going to be okay.

The Lazarus Story

Now a certain man was ill, Lazarus of Bethany, the village of Mary and her sister Martha ... So the sisters sent a message to Jesus, "Lord, he whom you love is ill." ... Though Jesus loved Martha and her sister and Lazarus, after having heard that Lazarus was ill, he stayed two days longer in the place where he was. Then after this he said to the disciples, "Let us go to Judea again." ... When Jesus arrived, he found that Lazarus had already been in the tomb four days. Now Bethany was near Jerusalem, some two miles away, and many of the Jews had come to Martha and Mary to console them about their brother ... When Mary came where Jesus was and saw him, she knelt at his feet and said to him, "Lord, if you had been here, my brother would not have died."... He said, "Where have you laid him?" They said to him, "Lord, come and see."... Then Jesus ... came to the tomb. It was a cave, and a stone was lying against it. Jesus said, "Take away the stone." Martha, the sister of the dead man, said to him, "Lord, already there is a stench because he has been dead four days." Jesus said to her, "Did I not tell you that if you believed, you would see the glory of God?" So they took away the stone. Jesus looked upward and said, "Father, I thank you for having heard me. I knew that you always hear me, but I have said this for the sake of the crowd standing here, that they may believe ..." When he had said this, he cried with a loud voice, "Lazarus, come out!" The dead man came out, his hands and feet bound with strips of cloth, and his face wrapped in a cloth. Jesus said to them, "Unbind him, and let him go."[1]

The Key to
Finding the Blueprint

Okay, time to get specific about the blueprint and discover what's in it for *you*. The biblical story you just read is the Lazarus story that's well-known. Now we will step beyond that story to discover another story, deeply woven into the fabric of the biblical one. A story *within* a story.

A hidden communication—a cryptic message—waits to be uncovered. Here is where we find the blueprint outlining the series of steps for healing what needs to be healed. The blueprint, however, like the paintings hidden under paintings, is concealed and you must have a key to unlock it. This chapter provides you with the key, giving you access to the information about how to recognize and understand the blueprint, and how to use its Six Steps.

How to Gain Access to the Help You Need

The secret to the Six Steps is to recognize this "other story" within the story and hear its personal message to you. How do you do this? *You interpret each character and circumstance in the story as having its counterpart in your own life and in the circumstances that surround your present challenge.*

Each character in the story, every word spoken, every place and object mentioned represents an aspect of you and your life. The Six Steps come alive when you translate the elements in the story into your specific situation and apply them to your own life. Only then, when the steps are personalized to fit your specific needs, can they be effective. This is the key to unlocking the instructions that apply to *your* unique set of circumstances.

This key is your access to the help you need.

Now you will learn how to use it. Begin by reading the following two examples that illustrate how it works.

This Is *Your* Story

Right up front, it's obvious that Lazarus and Jesus are the two most important characters in the story. Each in his own way represents an aspect of *you*. Interpret these two characters and their words and actions as parts of yourself—as parts of your life, as parts of the challenge you are dealing with—and you are well on your way to understanding the message in the story and applying it to your own situation. The application of the Six Steps will be unique to each person who will interpret the characters and objects in his or her own way. Here's a hint to save you time and get you started.

Lazarus in the story represents the current you. Invariably you will find that Lazarus is a symbol of your current difficult circumstances. Lazarus, lying lifeless in the cave, might represent the you that is encumbered by a physical illness, or the you who has an addiction problem, or the you feeling trapped in an abusive marriage. Lazarus could be your despair over your child's involvement with drugs. Or he could represent your broken relationship with one of your parents. Maybe Lazarus is the part of you whose dreams and hopes somehow got sidetracked along the way, yet still linger on, aching to have new life breathed into them—the loving, compassionate you who got buried under an avalanche of abuse received as a child, or the you who so desperately longed to go to a university but got buried under a lifetime of family responsibilities. Lazarus might be the slender you who got trapped under a mass of body fat that physically and emotionally weighs you down, and that you just can't seem to shed.

Whatever part of your life you feel is dead and needs to be brought back to life, any part of your life languishing in a "cave of darkness," *that* is your Lazarus. Right now, whether buried under a recent devastating predicament or a lifetime accumulation of hurts and disappointments, you are not fully alive. Part of you, like Lazarus in that dark cave, needs resurrecting.

Starting to get the idea?

Now let's look at the other main character in the story. Once again, we'll explore beyond the surface.

Jesus in the Lazarus story represents the "real" you. He represents your highest nature—the essential, genuine, one-of-a-kind *you*—the *you* that is unique in all the universe and the *you* who is able to express your uniqueness in fulfilling ways. The Jesus character represents your life as you desire it to be: the sober you, finally free of addiction, or the you who is respected and loved, or the you who has forgotten the negative past and is able to get on with a normal life. Jesus in the story represents the life you will experience when you free yourself from your problem and celebrate the goodness life holds for you.

To summarize the two main characters, Lazarus represents the part of your life that needs to be restored. Jesus represents your highest nature—the real you.

In addition to Lazarus and Jesus, other characters, places and objects will show up in the story. As you become comfortable with interpreting characters and situations in the story as parts of your own life, you will be able to recognize even those not specifically mentioned in this book.

How to Read Your Blueprint

Finding your "story within the story" by identifying the various characters, places and objects and what they represent in you is a simple technique.

You may want to first read the story's original passages at the beginning of the chapter, not trying to analyze, but just letting the words "sink in." Next, read the entire chapter. When you finish, go back and reread the passage from the story at the top of the chapter, this time making a mental note of the people and objects presented and what they do in the story.

Now you are ready to sit quietly and *let your subconscious mind take charge.* No intellectual evaluations. Just relax and "listen" to whatever surfaces.

Don't worry if initially you cannot identify everything or even anything. It will come. The more you patiently practice this technique, the more the insights will emerge—helpful and wonderful "aha" insights. Eventually you will see yourself and your story at every turn as you progress through the Six Steps. The more you progress, the more you will look forward to new discoveries about yourself and your situation.

Heading to Step One

As you read and reread the Lazarus story, some ideas and impressions will pop up immediately. Other times they can take longer to surface. Whenever you do identify what the various characters and objects and words represent in *your* situation, you will notice they usually emerge not from your analytical brain, but from your subconscious mind.

Things may seem confusing at this point, and that's okay. Without the proper tools, it is difficult to clearly discern a painting hidden beneath a painting. It is just as difficult to discern the uniquely personal message for you hidden beneath the Lazarus story if you don't have the proper "tools." So if things seem a bit confusing right now, please know they will soon clear up. The proper tools lie just ahead.

Six Steps
EXTRA

When we (the authors) discovered the unique and timeless blueprint hidden in the Lazarus story, we knew from the start that it was a completely different approach to transforming lives. While lecturing and teaching the Six Steps, we quickly realized this was something new—something that really could help people find the healing and peace of mind they craved.

Exciting, fresh, contemporary—it was obvious that the blueprint, ancient as its roots are, seemed to suit today's world. We witnessed the success so many people attained by working with this timeless blueprint and its Six Steps. We are also convinced that this process is simple to work with and can be applied to any situation. As you, yourself, evolve and progress through the Six Steps, you will quickly realize that all it requires is your continual sincere commitment to follow it closely and let it become part of your life. The degree of commitment you give it is equal to the degree of success you achieve.

The desire to change your life is not enough, because a desire without a deed is a dead end. However, a small step in the right direction is enough to get you started. A simple change in your lifestyle can act as a catalyst toward larger, more meaningful changes. Making these changes in your outlook, your thoughts, your actions will keep you moving in the direction that allows the healing of whatever needs to be healed in your life.

In order to help you incorporate into your life what you will be learning in the Six Steps, we have added an EXTRA, which consists of practical suggestions. The EXTRA can help you maintain your commitment to the Six Steps and incorporate the new material into your everyday life.

You will find an EXTRA following each of the steps.

A
Basic Tool

Changing your life by turning the "impossible" into the possible is infinitely easier and quicker when you tap into your *inner* wisdom. This is an aspect of you that is beyond your logical, rational and conscious mind. It speaks to you in the form of intuition and impression and instinct and hunches and a variety of other feelings, even dreams.

An effective way to hear this inner voice is by sitting calmly and quietly, and simply opening yourself to it. This conscious direction of your attention to that wisdom deep within is commonly called meditation.

Meditation, as we are using it in this book, is merely relaxing the body and calming the mind so it opens to an inner wisdom you already possess—a wisdom that always knows the best path, the best action for you. This "voice" speaks quietly and is heard only in the Silence, when all thoughts and plans and strategies for overcoming your situation are dormant.

How to Meditate

Try to set aside time each day for a regular quiet time of meditation. Make it a habit. Sit in a comfortable chair in a quiet spot at a time when you know there will be no interruptions. Close your eyes and sit in silence. Most important, do not try to think of a solution to your problem. In fact, don't try to think of anything. Thoughts will float by, but do not analyze or try to get rid of them. Just observe them.

One meditative technique that works is to become consciously aware of your breathing. Don't change the rhythm in any way. Be aware of only your breathing. This works well to keep idle thoughts at bay.

Make It a Habit

For the first week or so, it may be difficult to sit quietly for even a very brief time. Your mind, like an inquisitive monkey, may jump from thought to thought, rebelling at the unfamiliar stillness, but keep at it. It won't be long before the hyperactive monkey settles down and you are savoring this quiet time.

A good way to become familiar with meditation is to begin with a short five-minute session in the morning and perhaps another at night. Eventually increase these sessions to as many minutes as you feel comfortable with. Gradually, it will become a habit and a very helpful one.

Keep in mind that this is *not* a time to think about a problem or a solution. On the contrary, *it's a time to simply sit and be receptive,* not consciously thinking any particular thoughts. Don't expect answers to emerge during your meditation. They seldom do. They can, but not often.

Rather, they often surface when you least expect it. Sometimes it will be a spontaneous illumination. Or the answer may appear while you're daydreaming or even in the form of a dream. It might come as a feeling that slowly overwhelms you, and suddenly you know what to do. You may hear words you've heard before or read something you've read before, but which this time seem different and new and directed especially at *you* as if you've heard them or read them for the very first time. Whatever way these messages appear, pay attention to them. They arise out of your own inner awareness of what is *really* best for you.

Step One
Turn Away

Now a certain man was ill, Lazarus of Bethany, the brother of Mary and her sister Martha. The sisters sent word to Jesus, "Lord, he whom you love is ill."... but when Jesus heard it ... he stayed two days longer where he was.

The scene is a dusty, dry desert garden. The only movement in the hot air is the silent labor of the bees making their rounds of the flowers. Inside the simple house at the garden's edge, a man lies gravely ill. In desperation, his two sisters send an urgent message for help to a friend many miles away. The friend has a reputation as a healer. They believe he can save their brother, but this friend seems to ignore the sisters' desperate plea and stays where he is ... *for another two days!*

A Puzzling Response

It's easy to react to a grave or urgent situation with fear, panic or great anxiety. Our world tilts on its axis and everything seems to orbit around that one "bad thing." We can let it take over our lives.

Now contrast that with the reaction of Lazarus' friend. Not only does he seem to dismiss the urgency, he turns his back on it and continues with whatever he was doing before the messengers arrived!

People who read the Lazarus story are often puzzled by Jesus' decision to ignore the dire situation of his friends and wonder, *Why doesn't he go immediately?* The disciples and others with him certainly are mystified by his response. Here is Jesus, a man with the reputation of a great healer, receiving an urgent plea from his friends, Mary and Martha. They need him *now*. His friend Lazarus, their brother, is critically ill, and the two sisters believe Jesus can heal him if he will come to Bethany at once.

Instead, the famous healer—the person who might be able to save Lazarus—doesn't make a move. In fact, he deliberately stays where he is for two more days. Why? What's going on here? Doesn't he realize the messengers have already taken some time to reach him, and that Lazarus could have grown even worse in the meantime? Is it possible that he doesn't really care about his longtime friend Lazarus and decides more important things are happening right where he is? Or, is there something else going on beneath the obvious storyline?

Don't Feed Weeds

By staying *"two days longer where he was,"* Jesus established the first and most fundamental step in dealing with any kind of undesirable situation—turn away. Do not dwell on it.

Seem ridiculous, even impossible, in your situation? Here is why it is not, and why it is absolutely essential that you at least try.

Certainly you should act on things that need to be done to help your situation. That's a given. The lesson is not "don't act on it." The lesson is "don't *dwell* on it."

You don't get rid of a weed by fertilizing it, and you don't get rid of a negative situation by feeding it with the energy of your fears. The more you focus on a problem, fertilizing it with negative thoughts and emotions, the stronger and more stubborn it becomes. The stronger and more stubborn it becomes, the more it takes over your life. Dwelling on a problem will not get rid of it. Quite the contrary—it only increases its power. Not only does it grow, its destructive roots reach into more and more of your life, crowding out other more positive and constructive thoughts, just as weeds in a garden crowd out the vegetables and the flowers.

If you allow yourself to be caught up in the situation, you become a prisoner of your thoughts. When you worry endlessly about the problem and allow it to dominate your life, the situation itself is in control. You're not, and the more the situation is in control, the more helpless you will feel.

As you are about to discover—the good news is that your life doesn't have to be this way.

Danger—Quicksand!

Think of a man trapped in quicksand. As long as he keeps struggling in the quicksand, he will never get out of it. By struggling *in* the problem, he remains part of the problem.

The first thing he must do is stop thrashing about because that only makes him sink deeper. He needs something on solid ground he can grab onto to pull himself out, or someone standing on solid ground to lift him out.

No problem is ever overcome when you are bogged down in it by dwelling on it and struggling with it from hour to hour. You have to get above it, view it from a higher perspective. Hoping to find the solution to a problem from the level of the problem is a dead end.

It gets you nowhere.

By the way, what happens if a rescuer jumps into the quicksand to help? He, too, then becomes part of the problem. This is what happens if you have friends who are actually helping to keep you in the problem by jumping in there with you and constantly reminding you about it. They are slogging around in the situation with you, and as a result, you stay right where you don't want to be. These friends are no help to you from that level. No problem is resolved when you (and they) are looking for the answer in the "quicksand."

The solution to a problem is never found at the level of the problem.

Remember, the good news is that your life doesn't have to be this way. As you continue further in this chapter, you will learn the secret of how to "turn away." First you will read what you have to do. Then you will learn how to do it.

Translating the Story

How does all this translate into your own situation? Let's look at the original passages at the top of this chapter and begin with Mary and Martha, the sisters of Lazarus. They are the ones who sent for help. In spite of the graveness of their brother's illness, they still believed it could be overcome. So you might look at Mary and Martha as representing the part of you that believes there is still something or someone *somewhere* that can help.

Mary and Martha are likely to symbolize your own cry for help. This cry might be in the form of prayers, or visits to doctors or lawyers or counselors, or letters to insurance companies. It could be imploring your friends and loved ones for support. The act of reading this book could be a cry for help. The bottom line is that something very important to you is not right—is hurting in some way—and you are desperately seeking to overcome it.

So the Mary and Martha part of you knows things are not hopeless or impossible after all. They are the part of you—perhaps at this point it is only a very small part—reaching out in the belief that it's not too late. Something can still be done.

What do you make of their words, *"… he whom you love is ill"*?

Could they not be another way of saying a certain thing or situation in your life—something you care about and value greatly—is "ill," is troubling you. The "ill" could be your body or your finances, or it could be your anguish over the health or the actions of a loved one, or maybe a deep-seated loneliness? Whatever your "ill" is, it is serious enough for you to be searching for help.

And it represents some aspect of *you*.

A Message to Your Subconscious

Step One of the blueprint contained in the Lazarus story requires you to be aware of the condition or situation you want to overcome *without* elevating it to top position in your mind. Rather than dwelling on it, make the decision to give it an inconspicuous parking space in your mind and take it out for a short drive only when you need to work on it. Force yourself to turn away and go about your normal activities as best you can. We know how difficult this sounds, but others have done it. So can you.

"... after having heard that Lazarus was ill, he stayed two days longer in the place where he was." Clearly, the story demonstrates how important it is to turn away from the problem (*not* dwell on it) because this sends a subtle but powerful message to your subconscious that the situation, no matter how impossible it may seem, is manageable. It doesn't have to ruin your life. By subconsciously accepting this message, you have automatically opened yourself to seeing other possibilities.

We want to emphasize the previous paragraph because, if you truly understand this concept, you will be well on your way to a positive change in your life.

In essence, we are saying that intrinsic in the very decision to turn away from the problem is a critical message to your subconscious mind. That message is clear and it is this: *"My situation is manageable. I can deal with it."* Simply entertaining the possibility that this could be true begins the process of healing because it opens you to infinite channels of help and an infinite number of possibilities.

"But you don't understand what I'm going through," you might insist. *"Nobody could expect me to be able to turn away from* this, *when it's staring me in the face every moment of the day!"* You're right. Most people would probably not expect you to be able to turn away from *this*, but the Six Steps within the Lazarus story are not about what most people think or how they react. Let's face it, most people think and react in ways that keep the "ill" in their lives, front and center. (You've gotten this far in the book so, obviously, you are different than those people.)

Body-Wide Events

Thoughts are not exclusively brain events: They don't just happen in the mind and stay isolated there in a recycle bin. Thoughts create lasting physical changes in the body. Every thought you think transmits an electrical signal via the nervous system and/or it sends a chemical message via the bloodstream to every cell of your body.

Imagine! Thoughts are body-wide events that affect every cell of the body. *Every* thought is transmitted in some way to *every* cell. How else to explain the immediate changes in the body when someone yells "Fire!"? You don't have to see the fire or even smell the smoke. All you have to do is believe— to have the *thought*—that there is a fire, and the body immediately goes on alert. The internal chemistry of the body actually changes. Emergency hormones kick in to prepare you for action—either fight the fire or run from it. All this is because of a thought. How else to explain the feelings of love and comfort when you remember a loved one giving you a hug? It's all because of a thought.

The popular saying "you are what you eat" does not go far enough. The complete truth is *you are what your mind and emotions are feasting on.* You are what you *dwell* on.

Latent Energies Awaken

We want to be clear about this. To turn away from the situation does not mean to avoid it or to forget about it. (That would be impossible anyway.) There's nothing wrong with giving serious thought to and taking positive action about your situation. In fact, it's essential. Address it when appropriate. Give it your full attention. Work hard on it. Do what you need to do, but do not allow yourself to dwell on it. Each time you are finished working on the problem, force yourself to turn away from it and go about some regular, positive activities of the day. Fill a few hours with something completely different, even if you think it's frivolous or silly. Can't fill more than a few minutes? Fine. It's a start. Every minute away from the fear and the worry is a golden minute invested in healing, so do whatever you need to do to steer your thoughts in a different direction.

Fear crowds out peace. So when you turn away from a stressful situation, you re-create a peaceful state in your mind, and an infinite number of possibilities appear. Just as stars seem to appear at night when the sky clears, possibilities that were hidden by clouds of fear and apprehension present themselves, each auditioning for a role in your renewal. In such a peaceful state, you are better able to evaluate the possibilities and to judge if and how they can fit into your life. Latent energies are given the opportunity to awaken and do their mighty work without any conscious effort on your part!

Look, the spirit of life within you is biased on your behalf. Give it the opportunity to direct you toward healing, to bring you a peace-filled mind, and to help you prosper in every aspect of your life. Give it the chance to guide you in the right direction. Shift your focus away from the situation as often as you possibly can.

Fear thoughts bounce back? Push them away. Did they bounce back again? Push them away again. Take charge of your mind and push the thoughts away every time they insist on reappearing. Try your best to do this. (Your own thoughts are the *only* things in your life over which you have complete control.)

Some will call this "denial," but this is a different brand of denial, and it is precisely what you need right now. You are not denying the situation exists. Obviously it does. You are simply denying that this condition or situation will have ultimate control over you.

Really, this is more a release than a denial. The only power a car engine has is the power you are willing to give it when you press down on the gas pedal. Don't dwell on your situation—take your foot off the gas pedal—and you rob it of its power.

Do as Jesus did in the Lazarus story. Turn away.

Here you have that fundamental Step One, which will lay the groundwork for the other five steps to accomplish their work. First, let's have some specific in-depth discussion regarding how to "turn away."

Beware of the Bullies

Each day delivers countless situations from which you can successfully turn away. You can switch channels if you don't like a TV program, you can move your seat to avoid someone's cigar smoke, you can shut your windows to keep out the rain. Yet wherever you are, whatever you do, no matter how far you travel, you take your mind with all its thoughts and emotions right along with you. Wherever you are, *you* are there!

Step One demands turning away from a major part of your own self and, frankly, that can prove difficult to accomplish. Moving away from cigar smoke is easy. The smoker is not likely to follow you, and so the issue becomes a nonissue. It's not the same when dealing with your own mind. The negative thoughts and emotions will hound you, returning repeatedly unless you have repeatedly refused them space in your mind. Over and over they will persist.

Don't be bullied. Remember, your mind can hold only one thought at a time, so push out the negative thought by inserting a strong positive one in its place and do it over and over and over again. Basically, this is what psychologists call behavioral modification. Keep pushing away the negative thoughts, and eventually, they get the idea that they are not wanted.

Pull a Weed, Plant a Flower

As soon as you get rid of a negative or harmful thought, instantly replace it with a positive one. Imagine you are pulling a weed from your garden and replacing it with a flower. That weed would never be able to grow in the exact place where the flower is planted. Pull a weed, plant a flower. Pull a negative thought, plant a positive one. You are in charge of your thoughts. Your thoughts are not in charge of you. Your mind can only hold one thought at a time, so make it a good one. Keep pulling those weeds and planting those flowers.

In the Lazarus story, Jesus takes a few days before he feels ready to deal with the situation. He uses those days purposefully to turn away from the typical reaction to "impossibilities." You are now called upon to do the same. Only you can turn away from the situation and give your mind some space. No one can do it for you.

Consider again this critical aspect of the story: In the face of a critical situation involving his friend, Jesus remained focused on the activities taking place "right where he was." He refused to buy into the fear of the two sisters and the imminent death of their brother. He refused to be pulled into the negative whirlpool of emotions surrounding the situation in Bethany.

You, too, have the ability to do this.

The "Sudden Knowing"

Step One helps avoid throwing yourself mindlessly into the problem. When the time is right, you can deal with the situation. When the time is right, you can "go to Judea" just as Jesus did, and calmly but powerfully go about the next steps needed to overcome the situation.

The situation is not acceptable right now, and so you will have to be daring. You will dare to turn away from it because you know, deep inside you, that somehow everything is going to be okay; and in that knowing—that "sudden knowing"—everything shifts. You can let go of your fear and allow the healing to establish itself without your even understanding how. Simply honor your commitment to the Six Steps, be patient and trust, and let the creative intelligence within you work things out as only *it* can.

This "sudden knowing" is something you cannot force. At some point during your work with the Six Steps, the "sudden knowing" that your healing is in progress will come to you. It will come when you least expect it, suddenly just there, sweeping over your body and over your soul.

Trust it. Go with it.

Do not question or distrust the feeling. It is the spirit of life within you, making its presence known, grateful for the opportunity to do what it was created to do. Once you experience the certainty that things will change and get better, you automatically make yourself available to this creative power.

A Personal "Turn Away" Account

Roland and Sally had been married 53 years when their happy relationship changed. Sally developed Alzheimer's disease and Roland, devastated by the situation, became her full-time caregiver. We met Roland when he attended one of our Six Steps classes, in which we gave the students printouts of the material. He kept in touch and eventually sent us this letter.

I knew at the outset that Sally was not suffering. Yet after six months of caring for her, I was the one who was suffering—24/7 nurse, chief cook and bottle washer, housekeeper, laundry man, with no companionship and no foreseeable future other than more of the same. I felt I was at the end of my rope. I was desperate for a lifeline I could grab onto to keep me going—anything. When that blueprint with its Six Steps came into my life, it seemed like a miracle. Sally was doing well with the care I provided, but I needed help—lots of it and quickly.

Well, let me tell you, Step One just about made me give up on the whole thing. When I first skimmed quickly through that step asking me to turn away, I almost screamed, "What? This is for dreamers!" To even imagine I could ever be able to turn away from such an impossible situation was a joke—a bad joke. Oh, I turned away all right. I turned away from those Six Steps.

A week later, Sally sank into a deeper level of her private world, and my heart was breaking. I finally was able to get some part-time help to care for Sally. While it did relieve some of my physical stress, it did nothing to ease my emotional pain or the psychological distress of always being "on call." For some unknown reason, I decided to take another look at those Six Steps. This time the words about turning away touched something in my mind (or heart or soul or whatever it's called), and I knew this was the lifeline I had been aching for. I grabbed it like a starved wolf and greedily devoured it step by step.

Step One was the wellspring for me. The other five flowed from it, but without succeeding with Step One, I would not have gotten far with the rest, I can promise you that. I guess you are wondering how I worked my "turn away" strategy, so let me tell you.

I live in southern Arizona, where the winters are mild and sunny. Plants grow all year here, so gardens need year-round care. I was struck by that part in Step One that talks about "Don't Feed Weeds," and it triggered an idea in my mind. I used to enjoy gardening and horticulture when I was a boy. Why don't I start doing some now? So I did. I began by creating a small garden on the east side of our house. It felt right. After getting my own little garden going, I created and cared for the gardens of a few of my neighbors.

You might wonder how some simple gardening could keep fearful, negative thoughts away like pulled weeds, but it did because I love it so much that my mind found peace and stillness when I was in the garden. When I was working in it, my focus was on the garden, and so there was no space in my mind then for the worries and distress about Sally. I was convinced I couldn't do anything more for her, but I could do something about my own anxiety over her. I'm hoping you will understand when I say each weed I pulled was to me a celebration. One weed pulled bought me one unit of peace. I blessed each weed as I tossed it into the basket.

I also received a very special gift one morning while working in the garden. You know in the first step how it describes that feeling of "sudden knowing"? Well, that feeling came unannounced and suddenly swept over me like a shower of tiny stars. That's the best way I can describe it—a shower of tiny stars. There was no mistaking it. I knew, just knew, everything would be okay.

I can't say there was a "happy" ending to a story like this. Alzheimer's is too cruel a disease, but there is a "better" ending than the one I was headed for. I no longer have my beloved Sally, and I miss her every day. Long before she died, I was able to get my mind in a space where I didn't resent her, or her disease, or God, or my misfortune. When I was able to turn away from the situation, I reached a state of calm acceptance, and I stopped tearing my heart out daily as I had been doing. I was actually grateful that I was able to give her all the love and care she deserved. I am still grateful today.

A Second Personal "Turn Away" Account

Here is how another person applied Step One to an "impossible" situation. Marilyn at the time was one of our neighbors. We spent time with her and gave her a copy of our Six Steps material. She is a widow who raised her grandson, Paul. After joining the U.S. Army, he was chosen for additional training in Special Operation Forces. Paul did not talk much about his military training, and that made Marilyn suspicious, so she did some research. She found that Special Operation Forces are highly trained forces that engage in top secret, high-risk ventures in dangerous places. When Paul let it slip that he would be going to Afghanistan, she became almost paralyzed with anxiety. Day and night, her agonizing thoughts and emotions tormented her, and those who knew Marilyn could see the toll this torment was taking on her. The media's accounts of the suicide bombings in that part of the world, and the fact that Paul told her he would not be contacting her while he was on assignment, only fueled her panic.

Will my Paul be safe? What if he is wounded or captured or, God forbid, killed? Questions like these were invading every corner of Marilyn's mind, leaving little room for anything else. It went on for weeks and was getting worse daily. Brutally aware that she couldn't go on like this much longer, Marilyn became almost frantic to try something—anything—that might ease her emotional pain. She began her healing by coming up with a solid plan to "turn away."

The First Breakthrough

Marilyn acknowledged it was natural to be concerned for the safety of someone she loved so dearly. Paul was in a dangerous situation, far from home, far from the people he loved and who loved him. Certainly she was worried about him, but she was able to face the fact that worrying would not help Paul—and clearly it wasn't helping *her*.

Marilyn's first breakthrough came when she realized her need for some sacred moments when she could lovingly let her thoughts turn to Paul—sacred moments, away from the anxiety, when she could savor special memories and quietly be grateful for having him in her life. She needed quiet moments when she could picture him safe and peaceful, and feel he would be able to sense the love she was sending him. All of these were positive and constructive thoughts and emotions, whose energies would not only reach out to her grandson wherever he was, but would go deep into her own heart, as well. These were things she could do to feel she was helping him, and in doing them, she would be helping herself gain the peace of mind she so painfully needed.

Mapping Out a Plan

To secure those moments for herself, especially at the start of her plan, would take moment-by-moment attention until it finally could become a habit. What Marilyn had to do was try to fill up all the time between those special positive moments of focusing on Paul. She knew this would involve most of her waking hours and would be nothing less than a gargantuan process, but she was determined to persist. The answer for her was to lay out a daily schedule (very detailed) for herself, which proved to be an excellent idea because, in Marilyn's words:

> *… it was practical … something I could do. I drew up an hourly plan to keep my life packed with activities to accomplish. In fact, my schedule turned out to be so ambitious that I was too tired by bedtime to do anything but fall into a deep sleep. You can imagine what a blessing that was.*

Marilyn, a retired public school music teacher, volunteered to teach music to children of migrant workers in her county. She further explains:

This immediately became a delight I looked forward to three days a week. I loved the children and they loved me. When I was with them, I felt happy and discovered I was automatically "turning away" because I was too busy with the children to think about anything else. It was a fun time, but it was not enough. A lot of the week was still left unfilled. So I took a computer class, bought a computer, and spent several hours each day "surfing the Web," eventually selling lots of things on eBay that were collecting dust around the house. I can't believe I did this. Me, a computer nerd? In between time, I read one trashy novel after another!

I know this might not be a good plan for somebody else, but it sure worked for me. My mind stayed so occupied that anxiety thoughts about Paul had little room to sit if they came through the door. I guess they felt unwanted, because eventually, they pretty much flew the coop. Well, maybe not quite. I have to be honest here. The anxiety and fear did knock on the door a lot. I worked hard to keep them out, but I'd be dishonest if I said they had disappeared for good. I always knew those scary thoughts were waiting out there in the shadows, eager to sneak back into my mind. Yet I can honestly report I was determined to keep them away as much as I could, and most days, I was successful enough so the fear and anxiety could back off, and I could enjoy a decent part of the day. As a result, things were decidedly better.

Ignore Them and They Tend to Give Up

Marilyn was correct when she realized if you keep ignoring negative thoughts, they start getting the idea they are wasting their time. In other words, the object is to keep your mind and your life so occupied with things—*other* things, activities you enjoy—that there is not much room for the stuff you don't want there. Thoughts take up space in the mind. That, in a nutshell, is the very essence of how to "turn away." It's so important it bears repeating: Thoughts take up space in the mind. So come up with activities and alternative ideas to take up the space, and you will be successfully turning away from the troublesome situation.

Once she was able to turn away from her paralyzing anxiety and give her mind some positive space, Marilyn utilized the next five steps very successfully.

Step One was the step that made it all happen for me. Without the freedom it gave me to turn away from that terrible anxiety, I never would have been able to move forward through the rest of the steps and become the more complete person I believe I am today.

Marilyn wasn't able to obliterate the anxiety and fear completely. (Who among us could?) She was successful in giving her mind enough worry-free time so the spirit of life within her could go about its healing work. By the way, in case you were wondering, to Marilyn's delight, Paul did come back safely.

Fun to the Rescue

One final note here: For Step One to work, select only things you really enjoy because otherwise they won't hold your attention. Your emotions have to be involved. Roland genuinely loved and enjoyed working in the gardens. As a result, he never grew bored with it and found it enabled him to free up some space in his mind for the healing power of peace of mind and for other ideas to come forward.

As for Marilyn, teaching music to the children, reading "trashy novels," surfing the Web, and selling on eBay were all activities that could hold her attention because she enjoyed them. For her they were fun. For Step One to work for you, you have to choose only diversions you really enjoy, so they will keep you focused on them. This way you free up space for the spirit of life to heal what needs to be healed.

The Only Catalyst There Is

You will have to come up with ideas for yourself, of course, but once you do, you will be able to "turn away" and leave space in your thoughts and emotions so the healing can begin.

Filling your mind and hours with meaningful and enjoyable activities leaves little room for the negative stuff. Any (even the tiniest) amount of time you can keep the demons out of your mind allows your inner intelligence to come forth and to lead you in the direction of healing. Trust the process.

More than anything else, you need to trust in the power of taking these steps in order to activate the transformative power already in you. (Fortunately, understanding the mysterious ways of the universal wisdom is not a requirement, so why try?) Trust is the catalyst, the *only* catalyst, which begins the process of making the impossible possible.

Trust …

That 51 Percent Advantage

Let's be realistic. It's not possible to fill your mind with *only* positive, hopeful, happy thoughts and actions every day, all day long. Yet it is possible to have at least partial success, which is better than nothing. You can be successful at "turning away" if you can just manage to do so for the greater percentage of each day. So if at the end of a day you estimate only 51 percent of your thoughts, emotions and actions were positive, you've come out ahead. Then you can work on increasing the daily percentage of positive (constructive) thoughts, emotions and actions. Start by aiming for that 51 percent and work up from there.

Just for Today

Do your best today to ignore your usual anxiety about whatever it is that feels impossible to overcome. Just for today (or at least as much of the day as you can manage) turn away from those agonizing thoughts and emotions and *insist* on filling your mind and hours with positive activities you probably haven't done in a while. Rearrange some furniture, clean out a closet or the garage, visit with a friend (but only if you can stay completely away from "the topic"), play with your grandchild, watch a "dumb" television show, read a book you can get lost in, go window shopping, do a favor for someone—whatever it takes. You can do this.

Give Peace a Chance

Be creative in coming up with a plan, making sure to keep things as light and enjoyable as possible. Design a realistic plan you will be comfortable sticking with. You might even come up with something quirky; whatever it takes to keep you enjoying it every day. Spend some quality time creating the plan, because it must be effective enough to make you stop thinking about yourself.

Yes, work on your problem when you have to. Take appropriate steps to solve it, but when you are finished, refuse to entertain the problem. Push it away each time it tries to control you (which it will continually try to do). Get tough with it. Push. Keep pushing. Every day is a *new* day, and you do have the power to place yourself in charge.

Work with this step to get the feel of it. Stay with it until it becomes comfortable. Practice it every day until you can turn away and free-up space in your mind so peace has an opportunity to take over for a while. When you are able to achieve this, you'll be ready to add the next step. As was Jesus in the Lazarus story, you will be ready to go to Judea—your own "Judea," where the action will take place.

Passport to Freedom

You have read the personal accounts of how two people utilized the first step:

A man whose wife had Alzheimer's disease.

A retired music teacher whose grandson, in the U.S. Army Special Forces, was in Afghanistan.

No matter what your own situation, the timeless set of instructions defined in the Lazarus story can help. The steps are simple, but they do require your strong commitment to them if you want to succeed. They require letting go of the old memories and habitual reactions that have been keeping you where you are. Step out with unquestioning trust.

You *can* do it.

You *can* change.

You *can* cast off the old restricting thoughts and attitudes that kept the real you buried for too long.

Yes, you can. You already have the power to do this. You were born with it.

When you begin by taking this first step, you will be awakening a creative intelligence deep within you that knows not only *what* to do, but also *how* to do it. This power can heal, can harmonize, and bring peace back into your life.

It all begins by turning away and trusting ... starting today.

Centering Thought for Step One

How grateful I am for the gift of life. The creative intelligence deep within me knows what to do and how to do it. So I relax now ... I relax ... I find the inner strength to turn away from fear and devote this day to enjoying the simple pleasures all around me. I become a blessing to everyone in my life ... and I am at peace.

Step One EXTRA
"Turn Away"

Choosing your "turn away" time is your first step and an important one because it's a step you will be using throughout the entire Six Steps. Be sure to choose an activity so appealing that it will fill your mind and block out the negative thoughts that will be constantly competing for your emotions. You may have to run through several "tryouts" to see which one is *the* one for you. The more enjoyable it is, the more you will rely on it and use it.

What's Your "Happy Ending"?

Write your own "happy ending" story. Exactly what do you want to achieve? If your story were in this book, what would it say? It isn't enough to write, "I just want to be happy." That's like going to the ticket counter at an airport and saying, "I want a ticket to someplace nice." There are tickets to lots of nice places, but there are no tickets to "Someplace Nice." Be specific.

Set Aside Time

Remember that Mary and Martha were sure that something could be done to help their brother, Lazarus. Can you recognize that they represent a part of you? The fact you've chosen to begin the Six Steps implies you, too, believe it's not too late to alter your life and find the help you've been searching for. Once you experience the sureness that things will change for the better, you automatically open yourself to making meaningful changes. Trust is faith in action. Actively trust this phenomenon and you will have made a giant leap.

The Spirit of Life in you is always biased on your behalf. As we stated in this Step, "Latent energies are given the opportunity to awaken and do their mighty work without any conscious effort on your part!" When you turn away from clogging your mind with fears and negative thoughts, you are allowing these latent energies to activate and guide you in the right directions. All this is accomplished without your conscious effort!

Meditation will greatly enhance your ability to work with these energies. If you haven't yet set aside time for sitting in silence every day, now might be a perfect opportunity to prepare a meditation schedule.

Step Two
Remove the Stone

... When Jesus arrived, he found that Lazarus had already been in the tomb four days ... and many of the Jews had come to Martha and Mary to console them about their brother ... When Mary came where Jesus was and saw him, she knelt at his feet and said to him, "Lord, if you had been here, my brother would not have died." ... He said, "Where have you laid him?" They said to him, "Lord, come and see." ... Then Jesus ... came to the tomb. It was a cave, and a stone was lying against it. Jesus said, "Take away the stone." Martha, the sister of the dead man, said to him, "Lord, already there is a stench because he has been dead four days."

Several days have passed. We now find Jesus arriving at Bethany. Lazarus, it seems, has died in the meantime. "You're too late" is the outcry from the locals. "You could have saved him, but now it's too late. If only ..." How many times have you tortured yourself with those words "could have" and "should have" and "if only ..."? "Things could have been different now, if only ..." So often we squander our life energy paging through a litany of "if onlys" and "what ifs."

It sounds as if Mary and Martha have begun the blame game. (Aren't there times when we all try to place the blame somewhere else?) Because every phrase of the story has a personal meaning for you, see if you can identify what this particular statement from the two sisters represents in your life. You might work it this way:

Jesus in the story represents my highest nature, my highest wisdom.

Jesus was absent when Lazarus was failing.

Mary and Martha believed if Jesus had been present, the outcome would have been different.

Was my highest nature (highest wisdom) there to guide me when the present problem began?

Have a go at continuing along these lines. Without getting caught up in the literal story, see if you can identify how this part of the story represents an aspect of your own life.

Don't Play That Game

Notice that Jesus remains confident and calm, not buying into the negative "if onlys" and the criticism directed at him. He stays focused on what he has to do and asks Mary and Martha to take him to the place where their brother lies.

When they reach the tomb, which is actually a cave, Jesus encounters an enormous stone blocking the opening. Immediately he demands that the stone be removed: *"Take away the stone."* It looks as if Jesus is really rolling up his sleeves here, ready for action. However, this stone is no pebble. It takes a large boulder to block a cave opening wide enough for people to carry in a human body. Obviously it will take a great effort to remove it. Is it really worth such effort? What then? Lazarus is dead, so what's the point?

Not only that, did you notice how quick the bystanders are to call attention to some bad news (aren't they always)? Lazarus has been dead for four days, and as Martha points out, "... *already there is a stench.*" Something rotten is in that cave. Why would anyone want to expose *that*?

Yet Jesus, facing the prospect of what most of us might call a hopeless (not to mention grisly) situation, stands firm. He doesn't vacillate or complain. Without a trace of hesitation or doubt, he responds with a simple but direct command. Something extraordinary is about to happen, something he knows cannot happen until this huge block of stone has been removed and the rotten smell confronted.

"Take away the stone."

"Bad News" Is Good News!

Step Two in healing whatever needs to be healed is "Remove the Stone"—get rid of that huge roadblock standing in your way of overcoming whatever you need to overcome. Obviously, if anything is going to restore Lazarus, it is not going to happen as long as that stone is sealing the cave. Nor can anything be done to restore your life to wholeness as long as that stone is still blocking your path.

Now, no one can know what your own situation is or what this huge stone blocking your life represents. Only *you* will be able to determine that, but it's likely that *something* is obstructing your path, and that it's very big. Some aspect of your life is in a dark cave, and only you know what obstruction is keeping it there.

This may sound like bad news, but it is actually good news. It means as soon as you discover what this obstacle is, you will have taken a giant step in the direction of freedom. Only one entrance led into that cave of Lazarus, and only one way leads to the solution to your situation, and that one way is through you. There is no other way. Clearly, the stone has to go.

The Secret of the Stone

The key now is to identify and interpret the stone—*your* stone. What does it represent in your life? For starters, you need to know right up front that this stone is not another person or external condition in your life. It never is. Nor is this stone the illness or the financial collapse or the abusive relationship. In other words, the stone is not the situation itself. All of *that* will begin to shift once the stone is identified and pushed aside.

This roadblock is something within you. It could be a very strong belief, attitude or habit. It's often a memory that has been choking off your life force and preventing you from being a complete person. At some point in your life you may have, on an unconscious level, decided to confine your problem—wall it off from your life so it will lessen its influence on you. Perhaps you thought you could then get on with your life. Perhaps you encapsulated the hurt of a broken heart that you walled off so it's never hurt again. Of course, then the stone also blocked—and continues to block—the opportunity for a loving relationship. That's what happens when we wall something in. We are walling something or someone else out.

The life that should be yours cannot happen until this roadblock—this mind-set—is removed. The journey to wholeness requires a clear road.

So here's the big question: Are you willing to search through your heart and mind with courage and honesty until you locate and identify the obstacle? This could happen soon or it could take some time and patience. Unless you can identify the stone, you can't remove it.

With Friends Like These …

What about those onlookers at the tomb of Lazarus? Let's not forget about them. Consoling the sisters Mary and Martha, we have an army of so-called "friends." Surely these represent the crepehangers in your life who are always so keen to tell you how bad your situation is. Rather than helping you roll the stone away, they sometimes work hard to keep it in place!

"You're going back to college at your age?" one might say. "Don't be ridiculous."

"You'll see! That weight will soon come bouncing back."

"My cousin had the same condition you have and she never got over it."

When trouble comes into your life, it is really a good idea to choose your friends carefully. You want to be around people who support you, not those who keep reminding you how "impossible" your situation is. If you were going to climb a mountain, you wouldn't choose climbing partners who are afraid of heights. So right now it makes sense to surround yourself with people who are not afraid of spiritual heights, people who are able to view your situation from a higher perspective, and instead of rehashing the problem, can help you by concentrating on the solution.

Some Help for Your Search

Everything in the story represents something in your life, so what about the four days Lazarus spent in the tomb? Could it be that they represent the amount of time a long-standing problem has kept your life in darkness? And when you finally get around to involving your highest self in the solution (represented here by Jesus), by then the problem appears to have become hopeless (represented by Lazarus lying entombed in his cave)?

Do you believe there is a "huge stone" blocking your success in overcoming your problem? Do you believe the problem you're facing has entombed you in a cave for too long for anything to be done about it?

You will want to spend some time identifying how your own situation echoes the story.

How to Identify Your Stone

Once you discover the obstacle and become aware of how it is affecting your life, you will want to do everything in your power to remove it. *"Take away the stone."* Of course, you cannot remove the obstacle until you first locate and identify what the obstacle is.

Exactly how do you go about identifying the impediment that is blocking a more fulfilling life? One of the best, simplest, and most effective ways to do this is to sit quietly for several minutes each day and sincerely, from your heart, *allow* your unconscious mind to speak to you and reveal what this stone is. Earnestly desire to find out. Make this plea, silently or aloud, and in the stillness of your quiet time, *listen carefully* to that gentle "voice" within you. The answer is there. You may hear it in a time of quiet contemplation or it could be revealed in the form of a dream or it could just pop out while you're driving to work or washing the dishes. The fact that you sincerely want this revelation means it will be revealed to you. Don't try to force it. Be patient and it will happen. When it does, listen carefully. That voice is gentle, and cannot be heard over the cacophony of fear and worry that can loudly play in your mind. Yet identifying the stone is worth the effort because that revelation is a great help to getting it out of your life forever.

A Frequent Discovery

Often people discover the stone is what we call an "unforgiveness" bitterly hiding out in their hearts. Sometimes it has been there so long that it seems it has always been a part of their emotional landscape, and it can take an excruciatingly honest search to discover it. Resentment, anger, shame, guilt and blame seem to be the biggest blocks in our lives, so it might save you time and effort to begin by sniffing around in those areas. You might be surprised by what you discover.

If you do find an unforgiveness lurking somewhere in your heart, but you think it is not directly related to your problem, don't be tempted to pass it by. It *is* related. Unforgiveness is like an eclipse of the sun that brings darkness to certain areas of the planet. In a normal eclipse, those areas remain in darkness for only as long as it takes the eclipse to pass. But what if the eclipse were permanent? Then everything forced to exist in the darkness of the eclipse would eventually die.

Unforgiveness silently spreads its darkness into every corner of your body and soul. You become incapable of dealing fully with the situation because all of your emotional and spiritual resources are in shadows, thwarted and distorted by the shroud of darkness. Not good for the soul. Not good for the body.

We have a friend who divorced her husband two years ago but has been hating him, hating his new girlfriend, and hating his divorce lawyer ever since. The former husband now lives in Hawaii with the girlfriend, and the lawyer has long ago forgotten the trial and the settlement. All three are happy with their lives. Our friend, however, is still seething with resentment and still explodes in rage whenever her former husband's name is mentioned.

On a strictly physical level, hormones and stress chemicals released by such negative feelings seriously affect her immune system, to say nothing of the harmful psychological and emotional effects. As a result, the huge stone of anger, vindictiveness and unforgiveness is, quite literally, making our friend sick—which, as a matter of fact, is precisely what she affirms every time his name comes up and she says, "John makes me sick." John is surfing, fishing and having a good old time in Hawaii, while our friend is sulking and getting herself ill in New York—in a cave of her own choosing with a stone that she herself created, blocking her exit.

So a hidden resentment (or even an obvious one) might be something to look for first when you want to identify your stone.

Almost Like Magic

When Jesus issued the order to take away the stone, "... *they took away the stone."* He knew if he ordered the stone removed, enough people would step forth to make it happen. We don't hear anything like, "Hey, I know it's heavy, but see if you guys can move that stone, will you?" There was nothing tentative about his request. His *"take away the stone"* exuded confidence—expectation—that the enormous stone would be rolled away. And it was.

The same thing can happen for you when you order the stone out of your life. You might think, *"Oh, I could* never *forgive him for cheating on me."* Yes you can. Take away that stone of unforgiveness. *"I'll never get over the shame of what my uncle did to me when I was a child. I can't ever forgive him."* Yes, you can. Push away that stone of shame. It's not your shame. It's your uncle's shame. While you're at it, remove the unforgiveness as well. If unforgiveness is the stone blocking your release from a negative situation, you don't really have a choice if you want your life to change.

The opening to the cave is both entrance and exit. You are welcome to stay in the dark cave and feel justified in your passionate anger and unforgiveness, but then you must also be willing to pay the price of remaining in the cave. Hanging onto anger is *self*-destructive. If someone hurt you in the past, why let a memory of this person continue to hurt you now and in the future? Do you really want to serve a life sentence with no parole? As soon as you forgive, you take a major shortcut toward healing. Forgiveness can roll away that stone almost magically.

Many Stones, Many Roadblocks

As widespread as it is, unforgiveness is not the only possible stone, not the only roadblock capable of keeping you in the dark cave. A deeply-rooted attitude or strong belief can inhibit healing, as can a destructive habit or an overwhelming fear. Emotional scars, too, certainly keep us from wholeness, as do destructive automatic reactions. These are all stones that can block any chance for healing. Their destructiveness to our lives runs deep.

For example, it is obvious the emotional scars of people told since childhood they are stupid and treated as if they were inferior will affect their decisions throughout life. A "stone" like that is huge and difficult to remove, especially since these people often create a comfort zone by choosing to surround themselves with the kinds of jobs and spouses and friends and whatever else reinforces their feelings of inferiority. Perhaps not as obvious but equally as destructive is the self-harm inflicted when someone has an automatic negative reaction toward a racial group, nationality or religious denomination. The same holds true for living in fear by almost expecting to develop a certain illness or disease simply because one's mother or father had it or "it runs in the family." Can these attitudes, habits, reactions and fears be anything but large stones standing in the way of a satisfying life? They invariably block the exit of a cave.

When you want to find your way out of the cave, you need clear and accurate directions. If you try to make your way by steering through prejudices, resentments, fears, or any other negative emotion, you are taking your bearings from a broken compass. It's like getting directions from your car's GPS that receives its signals from a defective satellite. If your "internal GPS" is inoperative, you will always end up back in the cave where you started.

A Personal "Step Two" Account

Emotional pain inflicted on a child can last a lifetime. Alex tried to bury the shame and psychological damage as he grew from child to teenager to adult, unaware of how it was infecting every aspect of his life and how impaired he had become, as he shares here:

> When a former U.S. Marine officer sits at his desk and sobs uncontrollably for no apparent reason, well, you have to know something is not right. My work, my social life, everything, had become dysfunctional. I was in big trouble. I knew that. I'd been aware of it for a long time. And it was getting worse. That spontaneous outburst of tears sure was an alarm siren to me. Something had to

change. My life had become impossible. How was I going to fix it when I didn't know what to fix or what was wrong?

By some fluke of fate, I got roped into a three-day retreat at a friend's church in Kansas City. You two were presenting the Six Steps in the Lazarus story, and I thought there might be something here for me. When I got to Step Two, I knew I was right, and I was so excited I wanted to run out into the street and set off some fireworks to celebrate. I knew, I mean really knew, I would find my answer here. I would find what was wrecking my life. I would identify whatever it was and I would blast that thing into oblivion!

As I worked with Step Two, the identity of this monstrous obstacle in my life soon forced itself to the surface, and it blew me away. There was no doubt in my mind, no doubt whatsoever, this was the thing holding me prisoner.

It was Wayne (not his real name). *He was tall, good looking, muscular and vile. I was only 4 years old when he became my stepfather and not quite 5 when the horror began. For the next two years, whenever we were alone in the house, he forced me to do awful things. He threatened to beat me severely and tell my mother I was a bad boy, and said that she would send me away if I ever told anyone. So I never did. I existed in a prison of dread and shame.*

My mother died when I was 7, and I went to live with an aunt and uncle in another part of the country, where

I shoved those two hideous years as far away from me as possible. I buried them deep. As I became a teenager and enjoyed my life in my new environment, I thought I had forgotten Wayne forever. I graduated from college and then joined the U.S. Marine Corps.

What I never realized was that what I thought I had buried long ago was stealthily expanding year by year, until it eventually ruled my life. Those early nightmare years were still festering below the surface, and by the time I was an adult, the severe damage had me locked in its grip.

As I worked with Step Two, things started coming into clear view, and for the first time in my life, I felt the possibility of overcoming whatever the thing was that had been holding me captive. Wow! I took a week of sick leave from my job to spend full-time working on my personal blueprint in the Lazarus story. Believe me, I was sick—emotionally sick. I was useless and nonfunctioning.

To summarize, obviously my buried anger toward Wayne had been eroding my life, grotesquely invading everything I did. I had never been able to let go of Wayne and the unconscionable acts he had committed. After identifying this long-term seething resentment, I was able to realize all the pain and abuse were not about me. It was all about Wayne and his own deranged mind. When I understood this, I was stunned by how easily I let go of my hatred and anger.

Once I had identified what was ruining my life, I knew the thing was too huge and too embedded for me to get rid on my own. I wouldn't have a clue about how to break free of it. Well, Step Two guided me so unbelievably well that I soon was free of all the negative, destructive emotions that had been hiding in me, eating away at my life. I was now ready to start a new life.

I have to tell you, the change was so dramatic I thought it might not be real, and I went through a "crossing my fingers and holding my breath" period, which is not the thing to do, I know. But the change was real, and I went on to complete all six of the steps. Everything in my life has shifted for the better. For the first time, I am able to have a meaningful relationship with a woman, whereas before I was afraid of intimacy.

Now here's the real proof of what I call the miracle. I can honestly say if I were to meet Wayne today, I would not feel sick to my stomach with the old fear and hatred and shame. In fact, I would feel only pity for him. That's how far I've come.

Alex included a very important realization in dealing with someone you feel has hurt you: The ugly experiences you suffered were not about you, they are always about the dysfunction of the other person. The fact that Alex overcame his negative emotions toward Wayne (something he previously considered impossible) and felt only pity for him is evidence that he had accomplished his "miracle."

A Second Personal "Remove the Stone" Account

Many years ago, Helen had an abortion soon after graduating from university. The decision had been a wrenching one and, in fact, continues to weigh heavily upon her to this day. At the time, Helen confided in her friend, Molly, who accompanied her to another city, where the procedure was performed. Afterwards, Helen begged Molly to promise she would forever keep the abortion a secret.

Ten years later, when Helen attended her class reunion, she was crushed when someone mentioned the abortion. She fled from the reunion, enraged and heartsick about Molly's betrayal. *How could she? How could she, after she promised?*

Helen's bitterness and anger quickly became the dominant factor in her life. Everywhere she went, everything she did, was overshadowed by the resentment smoldering in her soul. This went on for more than a year. Her first conscious thought upon awakening each morning was of her anger and hatred toward Molly, and her last conscious thought before dropping off to sleep each night was of her anger and hatred toward Molly. Always there, always eating at her, it was affecting her health.

Helen knew she had to "shove the stone away." She tried speaking with Molly about her feelings, but that only made things worse when Molly accused her of being childish.

> *I really knew that for the sake of my own health and my own soul, I had to forgive her and let it go, but I didn't see how it could possibly happen when the hurt was*

so deep. All I knew was that I wanted it to happen. I needed it to happen.

The best I could do was to focus on the desire to forgive and trust that somehow it would happen. I couldn't do this myself, so I turned it over to the spiritual power at work within me. I still can vividly recall the exact moment a few weeks later when I absolutely knew, this stone would be removed somehow without my trying to make it happen. When I let that feeling take over in me, a strange thing occurred.

I went to bed that night, closing the window feeling the same old destructive emotions about Molly but somehow sure that unseen things were at work. The next morning as I opened the window, I suddenly realized, for the first time in more than a year, the bitter feelings were not there. They were gone. So gone were they that I couldn't even recapture them when I foolishly tried, "just to make sure." Well, there was no doubt about it, they were gone! In fact, to this day they have never returned. It's as if they disappeared into thin air, and I suppose they have.

I want to tell people about this phenomenon. If you have a hatred or bitterness eating away at your life, all it takes is a genuine wanting *to forgive. Believe it or not, that alone is enough to make it happen. Something shifts. The desire, the wanting to forgive is enough to remove the stubborn stone of unforgiveness. You only have to try it to see what I mean.*

No words could capture the sense of release I felt after working with Step Two. The next four steps fell into place so easily. I'm a new person now, and my life is wonderful.

Like Alex, Helen knew she should forgive but could not make it happen. The only movement toward forgiveness was her willingness to forgive, and that genuine willingness was all it took to start shoving the stone away.

This is a hugely important lesson. Please use it if unforgiveness is the stone blocking your path to wholeness. Taking the first step—*the desire to forgive*—will almost always lead to forgiveness. Just as it takes the movement of only one snowflake to start an avalanche, it takes only one thought of forgiveness to lead to removing that stone from your life. The willingness—the sincere wanting to forgive—is the Golden Key. Once you genuinely want to forgive, you can step aside and let it happen.

It's that simple, it's that effortless. And it's permanent.

Isometric Forgiveness

The decision to forgive is often difficult, and sometimes after you decide to forgive, implementing that decision can be even more challenging. You may have considered it but are just not ready to do it. You may feel someone has hurt you so grievously that you just can't bring yourself to forgive. That's understandable. The path to true forgiveness can be a difficult one, yet if there is a *willingness* to forgive, that sincere desire is almost as beneficial as actually forgiving and will allow forgiveness to emerge.

You've probably heard the term "Isometric Exercise." Isometric exercises involve muscle pressure exerted against a stationary object, such as standing in a doorway and pushing intensely against both doorjambs. Although there is no movement, there is a great deal of muscle exertion, and therefore, muscle development. Think of it. If every day you tried to lift your car, there would obviously be no movement of the car. Yet in spite of the fact that the car did not move, you would have strengthened your muscles more and more by just *trying* to move it.

It's much the same with *trying* to forgive someone. The difference is that no matter how you struggle and strain trying to lift the car, you never will. However, in trying to forgive someone, no matter how hopeless it may seem, as long as you keep at it and as long as you *want* to forgive, that "forgiveness muscle" will develop and you will eventually succeed.

Don't try to think it through. Forgiveness is not like that. Intellectual understanding alone can't bring forgiveness because it is the intellect that initially judges someone as unforgivable.

In 1981, a man named Mehmet Ali Agca shot and seriously wounded Pope John Paul II in an attempted assassination. The Pope suffered much pain in his long rehabilitation. Yet a short time later, he went to visit Mehmet Ali Agca in his jail cell in order to forgive him. The men sat closely together and spoke for a long time. When the Pope was ready to leave, he blessed Agca, and the two men shook hands and embraced. Asked by reporters what was said, the Pope answered, "I spoke to him as I would speak to a brother whom I have forgiven."

Did Mehmet Ali Agca deserve forgiveness? Perhaps a better question is, "Did the Pope deserve living with a huge stone of unforgiveness?"

Open the Windows

Keep in mind the personal accounts of Alex and Helen, who so successfully worked with Step Two:

A former U.S. Marine officer who had been unaware of how childhood abuse was impairing his life.

A young woman betrayed by her close friend.

Just as Alex and Helen did, you can discover the obstacle in your life. Whatever it turns out to be, it will always be tied to a very strong emotion. That is its trademark. If you don't experience some very strong feelings attached to what you think is the stone, it's not the stone.

After your inner "stone" reveals itself and you become more aware of how it has been obstructing your life journey, you then can take action to get rid of it. Let it go … let it go. Remove the stone. *"Take away the stone."* Make up a powerful statement, one that reflects your heartfelt desire to take command of the situation and that has strong feelings attached to it. Say it often. Say it with passion each time you find yourself dwelling on the negative. (This could even be as simple as a sharp "No!") Then get yourself out of the way so it can happen.

If you don't detect an immediate change, it's perfectly okay. Try not to impose rigid expectations on yourself. Keep away from feelings of discouragement and just know the stone *will* be removed. Simply insist again, and yet again … and again … if need be. Here are a few examples of a strong statement:

"I am worthy of love, respect and happiness."

"I forgive you. Forgive *me* for hating you all these years."

"Past memories cannot hurt me."

Those are just samples. Create your own statement that reflects what you want to accomplish. Affirm it many times a day, and expect it to work for you just as it did in the story. Keep in mind that you are working with the very same power that Jesus called upon in the Lazarus story. Let your statement be short and to the point. Say it with strong emotion, say it with great passion. Say it often. After all, it takes powerful feelings and a relentless desire to move a huge stone.

Open the windows of your heart and let in the fresh air. Is it really worth hanging onto and feeding the thing now that you know how damaging it has been? Think it over carefully. Isn't your own life—your happiness, your peace of mind, your health—far more important than, for example, nurturing an old grudge or a deep resentment?

Your Turn

The story has Jesus approaching the tomb of Lazarus filled with unshakable trust that something extremely powerful would take place. He knew nothing could happen until that great stone, sealing the opening of the cave and standing between him and Lazarus, was first moved out of the way. Right now, something huge is standing between you and good health or between you and a loving relationship or between you and inner peace and joy. Nothing can happen until you move that huge roadblock out of the way. Now it's *your* turn ..."*take away the stone.*"

Centering Thought for Step Two

I open my mind and my heart to discover the stone that is blocking my path. My inner wisdom reveals this to me in the perfect way at the perfect time. Yes, I am at peace—and all is well.

Step Two EXTRA
"Remove the Stone"

Have you been able to identify your "stone"? If you have not, the fact that you've at least begun looking for it will help it to emerge, so don't force it. Don't approach this search intellectually and try coming up with a psychological profile. Instead, just be genuinely open to uncovering the answer and be patient because it will come.

Put Things Into Perspective

It's helpful to remember, "… the ugly experiences you suffered are often not about you, many times they are about the dysfunction of the other person."

This was Alex's breakthrough realization when he was working with Step Two. It happens to be the breakthrough for many because it's so easy for anger and resentment to escape detection. They hide in the dark areas of the soul but, as in the legend of vampires, they shrivel and die when brought into light.

A lot of attention in this step was given to discussing forgiveness because resentment acts as a tether, keeping you bound tightly to the person you resent and not allowing any growth. Forgiveness frees you.

If you've discovered the obstacle inhibiting your life is "the need to forgive" and you find you cannot yet truly forgive, are you willing at least to try isometric forgiveness? Even if your decision to forgive was made at an intellectual level only because you know how destructively it affects your life, then start from this superficial level. A tiny seed planted in the most barren soil will eventually grow if not dug up. Start forgiveness from wherever you are, but start.

The Stone Disappears

Alex and Helen had each been carrying around the huge boulder of resentment for a long time. Such intense feelings can ruin a person's life, first emotionally and then physically. The enormous stone keeps every aspect of your life in a shadow. Thankfully, Alex and Helen freed themselves by the simple method of *wanting* to forgive. Genuinely wanting to forgive works, and without you doing anything further, the hardened resentment and anger disappear. A genuine from-the-heart desire to forgive can free you forever. Once the old destructive feelings are gone, they will never return.

Beware Secondhand Resentment

According to close associates and reporters who covered the Vatican, Pope John Paul II was never the same after being shot in the abdomen, arm and hand. Because of his severe internal injuries, he suffered greatly. Yet he was able to unreservedly forgive the man who attempted to kill him. In light of this complete forgiveness on the part of the one who suffered most, doesn't it seem strange that there are many people who are still not able to forgive his would-be assassin?

How is it that we can project our resentments onto people we haven't had the least interaction with? What are your thoughts about this secondhand resentment?

Step Three
Great Expectations

Jesus said, "Did I not tell you that if you would believe you would see the glory of God?" So they took away the stone.

By now, the crowd gathered at the tomb of Lazarus is in an uproar. The scorching air is abuzz with barbs and confusion. It's as if they are saying, "What's wrong with him? We all know this is an impossible situation. There's a body rotting and stinking in a cave! This man has taken leave of his senses."

Senses? Bingo! Things are often not what they seem.

Our five physical senses are relentlessly scanning for information to feed us. They are continually bombarding us with fragments of data that we collect and interpret. Our interpretations then become our "facts," but no matter what our senses tell us, we simply cannot trust them to feed us the complete truth.

"Seeing is believing?" Not really. The human eye can see only objects that reflect light waves between infrared and ultraviolet—a mere one percent of the vast electromagnetic spectrum, which means we *cannot* see 99 percent of what is actually around us. The human ear hears only vibrations that fall between about 64 to 23,000 Hz. A cat can hear sounds from 45 to 64,000 Hz! (Never try to sneak up on a cat!) Also, let's not forget our canine friends. Dogs can detect scents at concentrations thousands of times fainter than we can. So much for "seeing [or hearing or smelling] is believing!" The physical senses are inadequate monitors of what is actually going on around us and can never give us fully accurate or complete information.

Eyewitnesses to an accident or a crime are often certain they have the facts correct. Yet any police detective will admit how unreliable eyewitness accounts can be.

Think of how for thousands of years, because of the sense of sight, humankind believed the Earth was flat. It certainly *looks* flat, and so for millennia, humans relied on the unreliable. Still today we are continually being deceived by our senses. They do not always provide us with accurate information, and we tend to misinterpret and/or distort what our senses tell us.

Don't Rely on the Unreliable

As you observe your own life, can you see how your physical senses might be trying doggedly to convince you that you have a major problem in your life? Perhaps you've *seen* it on an X-ray. Or you've *heard* someone tell you. Maybe you can *feel* it in your own body. Whatever is threatening you is loaded with extreme sensory input, all negative—and not necessarily reliable information.

Fortunately, the truth is that you don't have to have *every* fact. Even if you did, these "facts" would be filtered through your fears, your biases, your preconceptions, the opinions of others, the often conflicting pronouncements of "experts," your natural tendency—like most of us—to prepare for the worst ("just in case"). Every nuance of information gleaned from your senses will color every "fact" you know. This is natural, but it also means that any "information" you have can be misleading and most certainly will be incomplete.

Don't stake your life on it.

Look Beyond the Five Senses

So why do we accept our sensory input without question? While undoubtedly our physical senses play a crucial role in warning us of immediate physical dangers, when it comes to major decisions and the deeper strata of life, where universal spiritual principles operate, we have to look beyond what the physical senses tell us and incorporate these principles into our decisions.

Why is this necessary? It's because we are more than physical beings. We have physical bodies, but we have a spiritual, mental and emotional component as well. So to base our evaluation of a situation chiefly on interpreted data supplied exclusively by our physical senses is a serious mistake. We need to look beyond the five senses for more information. Obviously this is what Jesus is turning to in the story as he ignores the grumbling crowd and silently watches as the huge stone is rolled away.

It is here in the story that Jesus reveals the crucial next step of the process: *"Did I not tell you that if you would believe you would see the glory of God?"*

Roughly translated, this says: Don't judge by only what your physical senses are clamoring to tell you. Look deeper. Become aware of the universal intelligence within you working on your behalf. Believe this, and expect great things to happen when you trust.

That is why we call Step Three "Great Expectations."

A Vortex of Power

Expectations have everything to do with faith. Every human being has faith. You may have heard people say, "I need more faith." They don't. They already have unlimited faith. What they really need is to point their faith in a different direction. No matter what you might profess to believe in or pray for or hope for, your actual faith is always invested in what you are expecting. What words, what thoughts about your situation are you repeating day in and day out? Do any of the following sound familiar?

"These horrible migraines will never go away."

"My son will surely go to prison."

"I'll never be able to raise that kind of money."

"X-rays don't lie."

"I just can't stop drinking."

Are your emotions pointing positive or negative? The simple truth is a timeless universal principle: *We tend to experience what we expect.* That's because our expectations form unconscious goals that continually point us in the direction of reaching these goals. It works in both directions. Good or bad … positive or negative … right or wrong. Expectation (faith) attaches as easily to a negative emotion as to a positive one. Unfortunately, faith in the negative is often more powerful because most people seem to expect more of the negative. In fact, it's quite natural. We want to be prepared in case the worst happens, so when a hurricane threatens, we'll stock up on radio batteries, food, water and even candles. We prepare for the worst, knowing that if it doesn't happen, there's no harm done.

Preparing for the worst and *expecting* the worst are not the same.

Expectations gather a tremendous vortex of power around them; an energy that draws to you people and circumstances and bodily changes that will support those expectations. Knowing this, you can see how critical it is to create strong *positive* expectations. Unfortunately, without active positive expectations, it's easy to default to the thoughts and attitudes of most of the population—the gloom and doom of cable news channels, the caustic babble of talk show hosts, the screaming headlines of newspapers, the negative buzz around the water cooler. These all fall into the category of negative faith directed outward.

You can also direct negative faith *inward* … toward your physical body, for instance. Psychosomatic illness (the ability of the mind to make a healthy body sick) is a perfect example of negative faith directed inward, and has been recognized by the medical profession for centuries.

That being so, ask yourself this: If there can be psychosomatic illness, why not psychosomatic health? If a negative faith can make a healthy body ill, cannot a *positive* faith make a sick body well? Yes, of course it can. The success of placebos is proof of this.

Living Proof of the Power of Thoughts

In the classic placebo effect, the simple belief that a substance will help results in a positive physical outcome. However, there is another phenomenon called the *nocebo* effect, which occurs when a negative attitude or expectation leads to illness or leads to some other undesirable outcome. In other words, believing that something will harm ... well, leads to harm. All this comes about by our thoughts and emotions.

Our thoughts about ourselves (our self-thoughts), when directed inwardly, are powerful almost beyond belief. Two well-documented medical cases are such extraordinary examples of the power of thought (positive as well as negative) that we just have to take a few moments here to describe them. They are quite unforgettable.

Case #1: A famous medical case on record reports a man who was dying of cancer, and whose physicians had exhausted all available treatments. The man had heard of a new experimental anti-cancer drug and was confident this drug would heal him. While bedridden and very close to death, he was fighting for each breath when he received his first injection of the drug. Three days later, he was cheerfully strolling around the hospital unit and joking with the nurses.

His tumors had shrunk by half, and after 10 more days of treatment, he was well enough to be sent home.

Two months later, while still in recovery, he happened to see a newspaper article questioning the efficacy of the drug he had been given. Immediately, he suffered a severe relapse. His doctors, in desperation, told him they wanted to try an improved batch of the drug that was far superior to the first batch. The man was ecstatic.

But the physicians had no new drug. They injected the patient with sterile water. The man, believing he had received a more effective version of the drug, improved even more than the previous time and soon was released from the hospital symptom-free. He remained healthy until two months later, when he again read reports that the drug was proclaimed worthless. In a few days, he was dead.

This man was so conditioned to believing what others thought that he could not even accept the *overwhelming evidence of health created by his own body.* Instead, he allowed his overpowering negative expectation—his negative faith—to take his life. What an amazing story![2]

Case #2: Contrast that story with this one from the great Nobel Prize-winning surgeon Alexis Carrel, who reported an incident he personally observed and later turned into his classic book, *The Voyage to Lourdes.*[3]

As a young physician in France, Carrel journeyed with a trainload of infirmed to the shrine at Lourdes, France. His intention was to debunk the reports of healing from the famous pilgrimage site.

During the journey, Dr. Carrel was kept especially busy tending to a girl named Marie, who had what he described as "a classic case of tubercular peritonitis." She was so ill, he writes, that her personal physician considered her case "hopeless."

While on the train, Marie lapsed into a coma several times, saved only by Carrel's emergency medical intervention. He asked another physician with him to examine her. They both agreed "she may last a few more days, but she is doomed. Death is very near." Carrel believed "if she gets home again alive, that in itself will be a miracle."

Yet Marie was absolutely determined to be bathed in the water at Lourdes. Carrel described her approaching death and concluded "… it was obvious that this young girl was about to die."

Marie did not die. Two hours after having the water poured over her at Lourdes, all symptoms of her illness had vanished! Carrel reported that "she was cured. In the span of a few hours, a girl with a face already turning blue, a distended abdomen, and a fatally racing heart had been restored … to health."

Again, an amazing story, but what a difference.

Beware of the Shifting Sands

While it's true that Marie had faith in the "holy water," her faith went much deeper because she could see that no one else who came with her was healed. If her faith were only in the water, seeing the failure of others would have been enough to crumble that faith. It would have been an intellectual faith built on the shifting sands of circumstances and appearances. When circumstances shift, faith shifts as well. Dramatic changes such as Marie's are never possible with intellectual faith alone. Intellectual faith by very definition is restricted to what the intellect says is true and the intellect, as we've discussed earlier, is based on limited information from the senses.

True faith, whether aimed in a positive or negative direction (it works both ways), is always based on a strong emotion and operates at a very deep level. Marie's faith did not fall apart. The holy water was simply the catalyst that fanned the flame of her much deeper faith. She believed—she knew—she would be healed. She expected it.

The cancer patient, on the other hand, had a faith that was purely intellectual. It was based *totally* on an outer appearance, which convinced him it was strictly the drug that had made him well. Even the powerful personal evidence of his healed body could not overcome his powerful emotional reaction to the negative news reports.

Then came the second occasion when the life force within him again made him well. This time with only harmless water! Yet his faith was so firmly rooted in the drug that once again he dismissed his own wellness and allowed the news of the drug's failure to kill him.

According to Your Faith

Aren't these two stories remarkable? Can you see that you always *have* the faith? It's merely a question of where you have placed it. The man doomed himself because he could not even accept the evidence of the life force in his own body as proof of his health, so stuck was his faith on something in the outer.

Here's what the two stories teach us:

To all outer appearances, Marie was fatally ill and *her faith made her well.*

To all outer appearances, the man was well and *his faith made him fatally ill.*

We all have the same amount of faith, but each of us invests that faith differently.

We tend to attract whatever we have faith in.

We can invest our faith in sickness or invest it in health.

We can invest our faith in hatred or invest it in love.

We can invest our faith in poverty or invest it in prosperity.

We tend to get what we expect.

What Do You Know?

True faith—the kind you can always rely on—is a phenomenon based on "knowing." Clearly, Marie had this "knowing." The question is, what are *you* "knowing"? Are you knowing that the right job is waiting for you? Are you knowing that wonderful blessings will come out of your heartache over a loved one? Or are you "knowing" your life will be ruined because your spouse is an alcoholic? Or that you will become diabetic because your father was? Or that you will never have enough money because your family has always been poor?

Plainly stated, faith is expectation. Whatever you strongly and consistently expect to come into your life is in general what you will tend to experience.

You have placed the order, and so the universe will make every effort to deliver it.

Is Faith Enough?

Before going any further, we have to note two important things. First of all, it takes work to move your faith in the right direction. It requires action. Second (and almost as important), although your faith is limitless, faith can only extend to the self-imposed boundaries of your present consciousness—your thoughts and feelings. That's where it stops. Your present consciousness creates an "artificial boundary" that limits your faith, and limited faith can only improve you life in limited ways.

How can your faith in abundant prosperity not be limited if your thoughts and feelings are saying, "I'll *never* be able to afford that?" How can you direct much faith in your innate wholeness if your thoughts and feelings are saying, "I just *know* I'll develop heart disease like my father?"

Faith is always going to bump into the self-imposed boundaries of your present thoughts and feelings—your consciousness. Faith can be invested as strongly in sickness as in health, as strongly in failure as in success, as strongly in hatred as in love.

Your self-thoughts matter. They matter tremendously.

What have you been expecting to happen? What kind of result do you expect in your situation? Take an honest look at the direction of your expectations, because that is where your faith lies. Where your faith lies, where it is pointing, is where you tend to be heading.

A Personal "Great Expectations" Account

A medical diagnosis can sometimes sear itself into our souls like a voice of doom. Douglas initially reacted this way when he was informed that the blood transfusion he had received after being injured in a car crash in Nigeria was HIV contaminated. Just one semester away from finishing law school, Doug felt he'd been handed a death sentence. Yet the story doesn't end here because Doug was able to pull himself together and realize he had other options.

He decided to take control of his life, starting with his thoughts and including a complete program of exercise and good nutrition, along with the latest drugs prescribed for him. Doug shares his story here:

> *Right away, I began to feel hopeful because I was tak-ing specific positive action. Just that alone was a boost to my morale, but the best part of my commitment to life was my solid "great expectation." I* expected *to feel strong. I expected vibrant health. I expected to be a vic-tor and not a victim. It took incredible effort at first to push away the negative thoughts, but my commitment was so strong that staying positive got easier and easier. Although I still am not able to dispel every negative thought that comes into my head, I have to say it eventu-ally became enough of a habit that it altered my overall*

perspective on things. Once I began taking your class, I expected to stay well, and deep inside, I knew I would.

I graduated from Step Three to Steps Four, Five and Six. Throughout those remaining steps, I found myself referring back again and again to my favorite—good old Step Three. I still use it and probably always will.

After being diagnosed HIV positive, I finished law school, passed the bar, and joined a law firm in St. Louis. I still follow my daily regime. I feel good, I'm happy, and I'm a true believer that great expectations bring great results. You want living proof? I'm it!

A Second Personal "Great Expectations" Account

Ellen's story is the story of a dream. A dream she had always believed could never come true. No one else believed it either. Ellen, head nurse in the geriatric center of the local hospital, loved the work that suited her so well, but her long-time dream was to be her own boss and run her own small nursing home. "Forget it, Ellen, it'll never happen" was the often-voiced response to her dream. The voice came not only from the subtle remarks from family and friends but, most important, from Ellen herself. Here's her story:

For quite a few years, probably 15 or so, I had this strong urge to start a care center, but I knew it was impossible. I didn't even know how to begin to enter into such a venture. I'd need a building, a great staff (that alone would be impossible) and more money than I could probably ever get my hands on. Okay, I told myself, Those voices are right. Forget the dream.

What happened was that, unexpectedly, the hospital decided to promote me to an administrative position. Well, they called it a promotion. A higher appointment they said. I called it a dis-appointment. I had excellent nursing skills and was at my best when I was with my patients. I didn't belong in an office anymore than a fish belongs on land. I found myself between an unrealistic promotion and an impossible dream. I could have looked for another nursing job in another hospital, but I didn't want another hospital because it would mean moving away from my hometown. Oh, boy. I saw my world collapsing. What was going to happen to me?

Enter the Lazarus story, with its six amazing steps for overcoming the impossible. Were they joking? They're looking to help the impossible? Step right up—I've got impossible. Anything for me here?

I had no time to waste and dug right into the steps immediately. Step One opened my eyes to things I never knew before and needed to know now. Step Two helped me get past the lack of self-confidence from having been told since early childhood that "you will never amount to anything." Step Three rang the bell. "Great Expectations" turned the lights on for me and allowed me to believe my dream was possible! I was so hooked on that idea of Great Expectations that I had to force myself to move on through the other steps, which I of course did. It was Step Three, though, that rang the bell for me—got my faith headed toward my vision instead of toward my doubts.

In the printouts you gave everyone in your class, Step Three contained a paragraph of pure gold for my situation. I changed the "your" words to "my" words and memorized it, recited it over and over, and made little signs of it to post around my home. Here's the paragraph:

"My positive expectations gather a tremendous energy that draws to me people and circumstances and bodily changes that will support my expectations."

I owned those words and I owned the great expectations they engendered in me. They so inspired me that as I started each day, I felt I was leading a parade with the right people and circumstances falling in right behind me.

You know, those words still give me goose bumps. Talk about vortex of power, I had a vortex going that to me was magical. I saw my dream becoming a reality beyond all my expectations. People seemed to come out of the woodwork to help bring my plan to fruition. Two skilled people appeared who would become my staff. Enough financial help came from an unlikely source, and I was able to convert my home into a small care center.

Today this private little six-patient care center hums along, just as it did in my dream. My great expectations smoothed the way and surprising things continue to occur, making the good things even better.

This Mysterious Force

In the Lazarus story, Jesus' passionate plea to the incredulous crowd at the tomb was a plea for understanding. He asked the crowd to look beyond the dictates of the physical senses and discover the great universal truth waiting in the wings to be acknowledged and called onto center stage. *"Did I not tell you that if you believed, you would see the glory of God?"* Well, there you have it! Believe, expect, and you will witness the creative process of the universe at work in your life. At work without your understanding how! Believe ... expect ... and get out of the way so this mysterious power can freely go about healing (correcting) whatever in your life needs to be healed.

You are redesigning your life. Be patient. Trust.

Train and Re-Aim Your Ship of Faith

You have just learned how Step Three changed two lives:

A young lawyer with HIV.

A head nurse who, in a dire situation, fulfilled her life's dream.

Turning faith in a new direction can be more difficult than turning around a supertanker in a narrow channel. Tremendous momentum has been built up and now must be redirected. You will need patience, and you will need to constantly remind yourself to point the bow of your faith in the direction of your highest expectations.

Be prepared to retrain and re-aim your faith. When the old feelings of fear or grief or bitterness come sailing back into your mind, rejecting them by jumping immediately to an unrelated and more cheerful subject works well. Try it. You worked on this in Step One, so you can use the same "turn away" principle here. A good plan is to have a few favorite topics permanently waiting on the shelf to be quickly grabbed for these occasions.

Enter the Correct Address

When you set out on a journey, your expectation is to arrive at a certain destination, a certain address. You might encounter obstacles along the way, such as detours and dead ends. However, if you continually head toward the destination you were expecting, you will get there.

A GPS satellite guidance device is a good example. After you enter the address (the goal) you want to reach, it determines the best route and guides you street by street. If a detour stops you, the system will recalibrate a new route and guide you once again to the original destination. The route will be different, but the goal will stay the same.

Whether a GPS in your car or your expectations for your life, you must enter the "address" accurately because that is exactly where you will be directed. So you can see why it is crucial to check continually on the direction of your expectations. That's where your faith is invested. That is the "address" to which you are heading. Great expectations lead you to great results.

Kicking It up a Notch

We can't leave this step without taking one more look at the passage *"Did I not tell you ..."* and see it now from another angle. What can this be other than your own subconscious mind (your inner wisdom) speaking to you, directing and guiding you? It's what led you to read this book, isn't it? If you had thought there was absolutely no hope at all, you would have given up looking for help long ago. *"Did I not tell you?"* was the silent voice in you, pointing you toward the solution you still believed existed, coaxing you gently to trust and expect that it will happen.

Continual guidance and direction from your inner wisdom is always set on the "tell-me-more mode." Tune in to it. Hear what it tells you, but remember, the subconscious speaks softly. You cannot hear it if you are tuned into the negative chatter that dominates our world.

"Did I not tell you?" Now you might answer: Yes, oh yes. Of course you told me. I am listening. Please, tell me more.

Treasure your inner wisdom and what it tells you.

Expect. Be patient. Trust.

Centering Thought for Step Three

I joyfully open myself to the spirit of life within me as it transforms and blesses me every step of my way. I fully expect the right things to happen in my life ... and I am at peace.

Step Three EXTRA
"Great Expectations"

Completing the Six Steps will not make something happen. Actually, you can never "make" anything happen. Of course, you can manipulate circumstances and events, and even people and give yourself the illusion that *you* are in charge, that *you* have changed things. The only glue holding the circumstances, events and people together, however, is the strength of your own will. If you let your guard down, even for a minute, the same circumstances and events and people will begin to drift back to where they were and, like a cowboy herding cattle, you'd have to round them all up again. It's a continuous effort that can wear you out.

What Are *You* Expecting?

Step Three, GREAT EXPECTATIONS, rather than trying to "make" something happen, simply *prepares* you to recognize and accept the right circumstances, events and people when they present themselves. Entering fully into this process brings a great feeling of relief, a feeling that help is here at last.

Asking yourself, What am I expecting? is different than asking yourself, What am I hoping for? As you read in this chapter, "Hope is unexpressed fear," and you certainly don't want to bring any aspect of fear into your thoughts. It is crucial to be clear about the difference between hope and expectation, because while a fear-based hope can short-circuit your success, *positive expectation gathers great energies to work on your behalf.* Your expectation is not only the direction you will take, but is the actual soil in which you grow and change.

Ask yourself, What am I expecting?

Know and Let Go

You read about the French girl whose faith was strongly fastened on the expectation of healing, whereas the man with cancer invested his faith in reports from the outer world. Plainly stated, faith is expectation. Whatever you *strongly and consistently expect* to come into your life is in general what you will tend to experience.

Make a thorough survey to locate exactly where your faith—your expectation—is pointing. Your emotions, your thoughts, your words and your actions are all part of this survey and, ideally, should all be pointed in the same direction. The more you can synchronize them, the stronger your faith will be in the "right" outcome. Simply know, let go, and then let the right outcome take its own course.

Step Four
Upfront Thanks

Jesus looked upward and said, "Father, I thank you for having heard me. I know that you always hear me."

The story continues ... the great stone has been rolled away. The crowd stands silent, all eyes riveted on the healer from Nazareth. The desert atmosphere is charged with electricity as, looking upward, he speaks: *"Father, I thank you for having heard me. I know that you always hear me."*

Hold on, you may say, "Giving thanks—for what? Nothing has happened yet." When someone does something nice for you or pays you a compliment, it's natural for you to say "thank you." That's being courteous. Thanking in advance is something different.

It isn't courtesy. It's gratitude.

Gratitude for knowing the right thing will happen.

Here we have Step Four of the blueprint hidden in the Lazarus story—Upfront Thanks. Sincere gratitude in advance.

Feelings Move Us

Gratitude, *true* gratitude, is not a courteous response. True gratitude is an emotion, a visceral reaction. So mere words of thanks are not enough, unless they can lead us into that *feeling* of gratitude. We need the feeling—the inner fullness of a grateful heart—in order to tap that power within us. Strong emotions will overpower an intellectual idea virtually every time.

Feelings are what activate the powers that make the changes and do the work. Feelings are the catalysts that start something. Feelings are the fuel to keep us moving. When feelings cease, actions cease. If you were sitting down right now, but suddenly wanted to get something from the kitchen, you would not even get out of the chair to walk across the room if you didn't *feel* like doing it. Feelings are the change agent behind any action. Only you can change your feelings.

Your responsibility then is to ignite the feeling of thanksgiving in yourself. This is nothing anyone can give you, or anything you can take in from outside yourself.

Life Responds to Appreciation

Sincerely expressing thanks unlocks the door to what might seem impossible. Whether dealing with yourself or others or even animals, when someone or something feels appreciated and praised, their best comes forth. Words and feelings of gratitude and praise motivate adults and children alike. Praising animals with loving pats reinforces their good behavior and encourages them to do even more. (Even plants are said to respond to words of praise by growing stronger and more rapidly.)

The cells of your body are more likely to respond and regenerate when they know you appreciate and love them. If you want more wholeness in your physical body, praise the evidence of life and health that you already have, because the intelligence within your cells will be encouraged to create even greater wholeness and well-being.

Do you want more prosperity? Give thanks for whatever resources you do have, and they will multiply in new and creative ways. Give thanks in advance for the good in store for you.

Fake It Until You Make It

All of this may sound good, but maybe you feel you're not quite there yet. Maybe you can't seem to get that feeling of thanksgiving. However, if you sincerely want to have a grateful heart, but can't quite make the jump, then fake it. We're serious. Fake it! Is this strange advice to give someone who is sincere about trying to turn his or her life around? Not really, because in this case, faking is valid and here's why. Your brain is wired so that when you consciously act "as if," you are actually creating new neural pathways, new ways for your brain to think. When you "fake it," when you force yourself to consistently think in a certain way and consistently "pretend" you are feeling certain emotions, your mind will eventually begin to travel along new pathways and accept those thoughts. This can then change your feeling and behavior, which, translated, means you are changing your life.

If, for example, you forced yourself to think in a kind rather than spiteful way about someone you resent, over time your hard feelings would eventually soften and ultimately be replaced by more positive, loving feelings. It won't happen overnight. Nor will it happen if you are not sincere. However, if you persist because you *want* to feel genuine gratitude, it will happen. Fake the feelings of love and kindness with enough willingness and consistency and couple it with a desire to want those feelings and, in time, the love and kindness in your heart will be authentic.

No Gesture Too Small

Not only are the spoken words in this section of the story important, the gesture is equally important. Note: *"Jesus looked upward ..."* A simple gesture to be sure, but very meaningful here in Step Four because it tells us he did not attempt to express his gratitude while looking at the problem. Jesus knew the answer for Lazarus (the restoration of life) was not in that dismal cave—not in the problem—and so he looked *above* it. What was going on in the cave was not important, so he ignored it. Outside the cave was where the action would be. As you discovered in Step One, the solution to a problem is never found at the level of the problem.

Use this technique for yourself. Forget the miserable cave that has held you in darkness. Look beyond the situation in which you find yourself. Look above it. Know in your heart that you, too, *"... looked upward."* That's where the solution lies, and the solution—the overcoming already on its way— is why you are genuinely grateful.

Think Play-Doh

Gratitude *in advance* is an investment of faith in the future outcome. You can't really feel grateful in advance for a good outcome unless you have faith in a "right outcome." You have an unlimited amount of faith, yes, but how and where you invest it makes all the difference. Like children's Play-Doh, faith can be shaped in any way you choose because faith is always wrapped in a strong emotion.

In fact, without an emotion, faith is merely hope; and hope, at its core, is unexpressed fear.

The Power of Words

Let's return to the story now. Note the words *"he said."* Why not "he thought" or "he reminded himself"? Because the spoken word is powerful, very powerful, whether you say the words yourself or you hear words from others.

Think of words that have hurt you. Maybe you overheard some cruel words not intended for your ears but that reached your ears nonetheless. Even if it happened decades ago, when you recall them now, they still sting—they still affect you. Think also of words you heard that inspired you or filled you with love or comfort. They, too, could have been heard long ago but can still inspire and motivate you.

Words are powerful, and the most powerful are words you yourself speak. Why? Because when you speak, an audience of 100 trillion cells in your body is listening (wow!), and the universe itself is waiting for your instructions. So when you speak with power and confidence, when you speak with faith, you are broadcasting your thoughts as instructions to yourself and to the universe: "This is what I want. This is my vision."

A Personal "Upfront Thanks" Account

Jim and Tricia, both skilled computer technicians, decided to go into business in their Vermont town with Roger, a successful salesman. They opened a computer sales and service center by investing all their savings in it and taking out a substantial business loan. Jim and Tricia taught computer classes and did repairs and consultations. Roger was bringing in the sales. Things were going well for two years until Roger suddenly disappeared with all their funds. Tricia and Jim were financially wiped out. Their story is a perfect example of "upfront thanks." Here's what happened.

> *Well, after the first few weeks of shock, disbelief, anger and you-name-it, we started to get serious about taking legal and financial steps to come up with a plan for getting us back on our feet, but we were ruined financially, and at that point didn't have much hope of a good recovery. The business really was dropping off without Roger to generate sales. We did try to make a go of it, but finally had to face the fact that we were not good with the selling end.*
>
> *When we were deeply depressed over our situation, with nothing on the horizon, someone (a former customer of ours) told us about the Six Steps and giving thanks for the right things about to happen. For some reason, we decided to give it a try and really got with it. The more we worked with it, the more hopeful we became,*

and when we got to Step Four, we knew we were onto something Big Time.

Every evening when we returned home, the first thing we'd do was consciously look beyond what had happened and give thanks for our lives and for the great blessings in store for us. At first it sounded kind of hokey to say those things, but soon we actually started to believe it. We believed that, despite what had happened, something good really was waiting for us. We believed this with such intensity that it became a no-brainer to give thanks for it.

One night as we were eating supper, one of us remarked at how beautiful our old farmhouse, Jim's family homestead, was and how lucky we were to be living here. We can't remember now who thought of it first, but suddenly out of the blue, the idea to create a bed-and-breakfast in our home just popped out! There it was, just like that. We were ecstatic. It felt so right.

We sold what was left of the computer inventory and got busy turning our home into a B&B. We knew lots of people start B&Bs, and many of them fail, but ours didn't—it thrived. Our combination of great location, beautiful accommodations, gracious service and genuine love for what we were doing all helped to create a very fine business for us. We give full credit to "upfront thanks" for bringing this into our lives. We still are thankful every day for our prosperity and our happiness. Had we never looked "above" our crisis, we never would have seen our solution.

What a great example of upfront thanks. If Jim and Tricia had stayed at the level of the problem, they'd still be struggling along in an unsuccessful computer business and resenting every minute of it. By trusting their inner wisdom and giving thanks in advance for something better, they opened themselves to that something better. They were grateful not only for the best (at that time unknown) outcome without attaching any specifics to it—no special requests or hopes as to what it should be. The moral of the story is this: When you look past the immediate situation, when you look above it and give thanks in advance, you dismiss the mental "gatekeeper" who's been keeping out everything that might seem unfamiliar, everything different than what you believe yourself to be.

Not a Matter of Luck

Psychologists agree but frame it a bit differently. They tell us that "lucky people"—those who "by chance" come upon opportunities more frequently than others—do so not because they are luckier than others. With these people, being in the right place at the right time has to do with being in the right state of mind. These so-called "lucky" people are more open and receptive to unexpected possibilities. They expect something good to happen, and so they are always on the lookout for it.

The "familiar" got you into your situation to begin with, so you can understand why letting in only more of the old familiar does you no good at all. If you've dug yourself into a hole, more digging won't get you out. When you can look *above* what's happening and give upfront thanks, you are inviting new and different ideas for your subconscious mind to evaluate and process. You are allowing the creative intelligence in you to guide you in the best direction, without your limiting things by wanting only what *you* decide should be on your horizon. The best outcome for you might very well turn out to be something you never even thought of, or maybe had never even wanted. If you are not open to it, you'll never see it.

A Second Personal "Upfront Thanks" Account

For something completely different, here's Christopher. His older brother was a Roman Catholic priest, and when Christopher was old enough he, too, entered the priesthood. After serving as a parish priest for 23 years, Father Christopher renounced his vows and left the priesthood.

> *I don't know where to begin because I don't know precisely when it started, but for several years, I had been wrestling with my doubts about the Church and my role as priest. Don't get me wrong, I had great affection for the people in the congregations I served and great respect for my ecclesiastical colleagues. It wasn't that. There came a point when I knew I didn't belong there. I had begun to question some of the beliefs. The more I tried to suppress my misgivings, the stronger they seemed to become. I felt invaded by the demons of doubt that taunted and haunted me. I anguished over my hypocrisy—saying the Mass when I didn't believe the*

words coming out of my mouth. What was I doing? If there is such a thing as dark night of the soul, I was in it.

I should explain that I have always considered myself to be a spiritual person, and still do, but I came to realize I am not a religious person. There is a difference. The only choice for me was to leave the priesthood. The day I walked away from the Church was a sorrowful day for my brother and parents, and thus an agonizing day for me. However, it was also a day of new hope, a new life to live. Do you know why? It was because I had just been introduced to a concept completely new to me—Upfront Thanks.

There I was, bombarded on all sides by "How could you? You'll suffer in hell for this" and "What are you going to do now? Better rethink this—quickly, before it's too late." Yet I was hardly affected by these remarks because I was enchanted (yes, I do feel that's the appropriate word) by the idea of being grateful for my life, knowing it would only be better. "Upfront Thanks" became my mantra. The joy and the sense of release I got from this concept bore me through that fragile transition period. I was grateful.

The outcome? Let me report that I am now a social worker, loving my work and happier than I've ever been. Here's the kicker. Two evenings a week I play jazz piano in an upscale cocktail lounge, where I'm billed as "Father Chris." Can you believe it?

When I left the Church, I knew it would be for a life of helping others in some way, and that's exactly what I am doing. In my heart, I believe my work and my music contribute more than anything I could ever have done as a priest.

Father Chris's mantra of "Upfront Thanks" opened the way for him to step into the right career at the right time. Here again, the perfect outcome unfolded because Christopher was open to (and grateful for) the right direction, wherever it would take him. Those words "wherever it would take him" are important because you can never be disappointed if your only goal is happiness and not some form of a specific "must-have" outcome you feel is the only outcome that can make you happy.

Are You Willing?

While it is true that the life force is always on your side, eager to work through you to heal whatever needs to be healed and restored, you have been given the gift of free will. So it is up to you to issue the invitation. It is up to you to show a willingness to work with this mighty force.

How do you invite an invisible, intangible power you cannot even define to become active in your life? You do it through gratitude, by adopting a mind-set of continuous appreciation for the presence of this power as it works through you, and an overall attitude of thanks for the extraordinary things that are going to take place as a result of your grateful expectation. Wonderful things, unexpected things, *right* things!

"... I thank you for having heard me. I know that you always hear me." This is the absolute truth. That spirit of life within

you is always listening, always waiting to become active in your life.

Common courtesy, thanks *after* the fact, has no effect on the spirit of life. Great expectation, along with a perpetually grateful heart *before* the fact, is what Step Four is about. This is what opens the channels. This is what is always "heard" by the cells of your body that are always listening and know how to heal; heard by the invisible forces of the universe ever waiting to fulfill your expectations. If you speak the words (aloud or in your heart), you will be heard.

So, from the heart, be grateful—not for what you hope it will get you, but for the utter joy that comes from acknowledging the life force at work in your life and from allowing it to heal what needs to be healed.

"Yeah, but Will It Work for Me?"

Remember the accounts of Step Four, the key to getting out of the cave:

The husband and wife in financial collapse who are loving their new career.

A despairing priest who followed his heart without losing his soul.

As you work through these steps, you might find yourself with feelings such as, *I believe in these principles in theory, but will they work for me?* When you are required to think and act in new ways, you can often question and doubt. To stay in the same old patterns, to travel the same old roads, often seems like the easiest way. However, the familiar "easiest" way turns out to be the most difficult because when you travel that same old road, you end up in the same old place.

If you have doubts or disbelief about the Six Steps, please don't give up now. Remain sincere and steady in your commitment to emerge from that dark night of the soul. Do your utmost to give these Six Steps a fair chance.

Emerson said, "Once you make a decision, the universe conspires to make it happen." And why not? The universal creative intelligence living in you and as you is *always* on your side, *always* working on your behalf. This spirit of life requires only two things of you—your invitation to let it work through you and your expectation that it *will*. Because you are working with a universal principle here, this power has no choice but to respond. Like a gentle river of healing, it will carry you along when you do *your* part and surrender yourself to its flow.

Trust the spirit of life. Be grateful it knows what is best for you and is leading you there.

Centering Thought for Step Four

My heart overflows with gratitude for the life force at work in my body and in my soul. I center my thoughts on the positive changes taking place right now—and I am at peace.

Step Four EXTRA
"Upfront Thanks"

Let's analyze further a sliver of the quote we are dealing with in this step. *"… I thank you for having heard me. I know that you always hear me."*

A Self-Fulfilling Prophesy

Step Four deals with Upfront Thanks and, yes, this phrase certainly shows gratitude, but it also shows faith: Faith that the words were not only heard in the past, *"… I thank you for* having *heard me,"* but also faith that the words are being heard in the present and will be heard in the future as well, *"… you* always *hear me."* With such strong faith, it is easy to be grateful, and therefore, it is natural to give thanks. Each time you give thanks, you strengthen your expectation of success, and each time you strengthen your expectation of success, you naturally give thanks. This, then, becomes a positive feedback loop, and gratitude for the good to come in the future becomes a self-fulfilling prophesy.

You may not be able to give sincere thanks in advance right now. However, in Step Three you worked on your expectation, so now you can begin to embrace more fully that expectation. The more clearly you can visualize it and the more securely you can embrace it, the more you will be able to express sincere gratitude in advance for its expression in your life.

Thanks in advance without faith is either an attempt at manipulation or the sincerest form of insincerity! Give thanks daily for what you can expect, what you can believe, even as you work on expanding that belief.

He Looked Upward

What are you thankful for? No doubt you could make a list of things that you are grateful to have in your life. There is always something, usually many things. More to the point for this step, however, is to be grateful for a future good that you haven't yet seen. This can be a real challenge if there is a situation in your life that you cannot look past. Perhaps you can't even imagine getting past the problem. If you cannot look past it, then look above it. The solution to any problem is never found in the problem itself. "Jesus looked *upward*," in the direction of the solution.

Look upward, give thanks. Do it with a grateful heart and do it often.

Prayer vs. Meditation

A note here to clarify the difference between prayer and meditation: You just read the suggestion to "Look upward, give thanks. Do it with a grateful heart and do it often." Doing this is important and is focused on your gratitude. Doing this can bring a wonderful sense of joy and assurance. Doing this can be called praying.

Meditation, on the other hand, is sitting quietly with no focused thoughts, leaving yourself open for the feeling of peace and perhaps a sense of the connection with your inner awareness. In prayer, you are sending out thoughts and emotions. In meditation, you are receiving peace and comfort and possibly ideas and guidance.

Step Five

A Strong Command

… he cried with a loud voice, "Lazarus, come out!"

We have arrived at a critical moment—the penultimate step of the Lazarus story. The great stone has been removed and no longer looms at the gaping mouth of the cave. An incredible drama is poised, ready to begin, the curtain is about to rise. The powerful voice of Jesus slices through the thick tension of the moment and loudly commands, *"Lazarus, come out!"* Right on cue, Lazarus enters center stage.

Let's move in closer. We have some key words here, words that reveal the secret to what *you* can accomplish. First, we have the highly significant phrase "… *cried with a loud voice."* No meek, unsure, timid, hesitant man, this Jesus, as he stands before the open tomb this day. He mobilizes the full volume of his voice and cries out—shouts out—when he commands Lazarus to come forth. Not with a whisper but a roar does he hurl his words into that cave. We can only imagine how the power within every atom of his body is emblazoned on these words as they travel into the tomb where Lazarus lies.

Volume + Power = Success

In the Lazarus story, the volume and the power of his voice are what ignite Jesus' words. If his voice were tinged with even the slightest hint of self-doubt or weakness, it would not matter *what* words he spoke. They would be useless, and the event would never take place. However, he is filled with absolute faith in what he plans to accomplish, and so his words are charged with an inexplicable force. Jesus, when calling forth Lazarus, is simultaneously calling forth the spirit of life within Lazarus. He knows it will not fail.

"*... with a loud voice*" instructs you to do the same. Speak your words of healing loudly, as much for others to hear as for you. If you have been telling yourself the bad news for a long time, now is the time to speak out loudly the *good* news. Infuse your words with as much power and heartfelt emotion as you possibly can. Something said boldly in a strong voice implies a feeling of assurance. When you're not sure of something, you tend to mumble it, whereas anything said loudly is something you want to be heard, right? So Step Five requires you to speak loudly.

A Silent Shout

Shouting aloud may not always be appropriate or possible. Shouting silently in your mind and heart will work just as well if you do it boldly and with confidence. Hear your words resonate throughout your mind, throughout your body. Feel them echoing in the chambers of your heart and in the spaces between the trillions of cells of your body. Hurl those words as audaciously as Jesus did in the Lazarus story.

Others may not hear them, but your own soul will. The spirit of life within you will hear them and will help you step forth into the light just as surely as the life force within Lazarus was activated to lead him out of that cave. Yes, words sent forth with authority and passion can operate in silence, and the result will be just as dramatic.

Shedding Some Light on Light

Before dealing with the specific words *"Lazarus, come out!"* let's spend some time looking at the power of words in general. As a good analogy, we can contrast the power of laser light to sunlight. Understanding this analogy will help you appreciate the power of your words.

The sun's rays are utterly universal in their radiance. They beam out in all directions, flooding anything in their path, lighting up the entire outdoors. Lightbulbs are similar. Their rays travel in all directions at once, indiscriminately lighting an entire area. Even a tiny candle will send its flickering rays in all directions. This is true of all conventional light. Even the most focused spotlight will still shed a bit of light in surrounding areas, spreading its light even wider the further it extends from its source.

Laser light, however, is different from conventional light. Rather than scattering in all directions, the light particles are all traveling in exactly the same direction. They are "in phase" with each other. This increases their power enormously. Light from a laser is powerful enough to burn a hole through a piece of steel, yet can be rendered "tame" enough to use in eye surgery.

Laser light is extraordinary—incredibly precise in its focus, singularly powerful in its effect.

Words Can Kill or Cure

Words are the lasers of human thought—incredibly precise in their focus, singularly powerful in their effect. Rather than scattering in all directions (like conventional light), thoughts expressed as words are in phase with each other, all going in the same direction.

Because thoughts initiate all changes, they are supreme as the molders of your world. Something else happens when you put your thoughts into sentences. When thoughts join together, when they focus and express as words, they take on additional power.

When you actually *speak* the word, it sets up potent vibrations in your body. Speaking and hearing and feeling your thoughts will always impress them on you more fully than merely thinking them. Words move you into action. When you declare your thoughts by speaking them, every atom of you body responds to the sound of your voice. Not only do you *hear* what you say, you actually *feel* what you say.

Every word has an effect. The intensity of the effect depends on the intensity of the thought and feeling behind the word as well as the way you speak it. For example, watch a tennis player aggressively and loudly encourage herself before trying to score an important point. Listen to any athlete loudly motivate himself to do better, or to scold himself loudly for making a "dumb" mistake. No doubt you've said some loud words to yourself on numerous occasions.

Another aspect of the power of words is that soothing words create the release of "soothing" chemicals in the body. This is true not only for the speaker of the words but also for the one to whom they are spoken. Angry words, on the other hand, trigger the release of harmful "fight or flight" chemicals. Again, this happens not only in the person delivering the angry words, but in the one receiving them. If you have ever spoken soothing words to a frightened child or remember hearing them spoken to you, you know the power of loving thoughts expressed as words. Conversely, if you've ever spoken harshly or been spoken to harshly, you know the power of angry thoughts expressed as words.

Every word you speak is saturated with energy that will create or destroy. You cannot help becoming what you consistently say you are. In a very real way, the word becomes flesh. It dwells in you—and *as* you. The more resolutely and intensely you speak words of what you are and who you are, the more surely you move toward becoming what you are saying. Also, if you choose to accept the words directed to you by other people—if you internalize *their* words as *your* words—then you will move in that direction.

Like an Old Cart Horse

Without a doubt, all words affect you, but it is your own words that affect you the most. Whether joking or serious, your words have impact. The subconscious mind has no sense of humor. The subconscious is like an old cart horse which thinks "giddy-up" means "get going." The horse doesn't know if you're joking or serious. All it knows is that when it hears those words, it is time to obey.

Like the horse, your subconscious doesn't know the difference between your constantly saying to yourself "I'm so stupid" and your actually believing that you *are* stupid. It automatically follows your command—your words. So *acting* as if you're stupid and believing, for example, that you're not smart enough to get a well-paying job or go back to school, your beliefs eventually become a reality.

Words Are Mirrors

The words you use reflect your state of consciousness, but they are more than that. They are the very cause of your maintaining that consciousness. So if you tell yourself, I messed up again; I really am worthless, you are not only affirming your present sense of self-worth, you are setting the parameters of your worth for the future, because today's words become tomorrow's reality.

For instance, to constantly lament in the midst of an economic recession that "I'm really worried about my money. I just know I'm going to get laid off and lose everything," is to focus on lack and fear. Such words crystallize your negative thoughts and are likely to bring about what you fear the most.

Think of the laser. The power of the laser is in its coherence. All light particles are in phase and all are traveling in exactly the same direction. If you want health and prosperity in your world, speak only words of health and prosperity. If you want love in your world, focus on speaking words of love. This is not a denial of the fact that health and prosperity and love might be somewhat lacking in your world. On the contrary, it is simply declaring to the universe and to yourself just exactly what you want.

When the great Hall of Fame golfer Gary Player was beginning his career, he would look at himself intently in the mirror and loudly proclaim, "You're the greatest golfer in the world." It didn't matter if he had just lost a tournament. He did not dwell on the loss. He focused on the great potential he knew he had.

Your Words, Your Life

An ancient Buddhist story tells of a wise teacher who was walking through a forest with his students when they came upon the partially decomposed carcass of a deer. The students, hoping to protect their teacher from such a repulsive sight, tried to steer him around it. The teacher, however, would not alter his direction. When he came upon the deer, he looked it over carefully and declared, "My, what beautiful antlers." He didn't focus on the decomposed flesh but rather on the noble antlers. He chose to look beyond the obvious and express the beauty. His words were not of repulsion but of loveliness.

You can do the same. Certainly you can find enough ugliness if you care to look for it, but there is also an abundance of beauty. Which do you want in your world? The words you speak will go a long way in determining which it will be. They become part of your new design.

Aiming the Focus

Now back to the Lazarus story and the command itself. *"Lazarus, come out!"*

These words, loaded with Jesus' conviction and his dynamic energy, become a command so powerful it can awaken the dead! First, notice he calls to his friend by name. *"Lazarus"* becomes the head of an arrow piercing the darkness of the cave and directing itself with laser-like precision to the man lying within it. "This is for *you*, Lazarus. Hear me. Hear me now!" By calling out the name of Lazarus, Jesus identifies the object of his command and aims his complete focus upon it. In this same way, you will be calling out your own name to give focus to your command.

Next, once he focuses his voice and his energies on Lazarus, Jesus boldly commands him to come out of the cave. Get out of that dark and lifeless place, Lazarus, and step forth into the light. When strong commands are issued with complete expectation, situations are made to comply. Lazarus walks out of the tomb!

Your Own Personal Lazarus

You may be thinking, *That was Jesus doing those miraculous things. Easy for him, but I'm not Jesus.* Remember the premise of this book: You don't have to believe the story is true in order to understand and utilize the valuable lessons it teaches. If you are experiencing a dark cave of your own, engulfed by some impossible situation, in a way you are much like Lazarus—dormant and needing to be brought back to life. By employing the same Six Steps that in the story Jesus used to create the Lazarus event, you can create your own "resurrection." How marvelous to know these Six Steps will work for you no matter what your perspective of the Lazarus story is. The blueprint stands independent from all opinions and beliefs about the story.

Step Five of the blueprint hidden in the Lazarus story is A Strong Command—a forceful, passionate, faith-filled command to the life force dormant within you to awaken and "come out!" From the very pinnacle of your higher self, call out your name and command yourself to step forth into the light saturated with new life. Every cell, every thought, every emotion can be transformed and made new. Demand it. *Command* it. Feel in your heart the power of your command. Hear it resounding through your body.

You might want to use something similar to:

(Your name), you are healed and restored to life. Come out in the light now!

(Your name), you are free and ready to start a new life. Come out now!

(Your name), wake up to your new self. Wake up filled with peace. Come out now!

(Your name), no substance can control you. You are in charge. Come out now!

Make your commands sharp and incisive. Can you imagine trying to chop down a tree with the broad side of an axe? Of course not. You aim the sharp cutting edge directly at the trunk. Likewise, you cannot break out of a psychological cave with broad, mealy-mouthed wishes. That won't work either.

You have to issue a sharp command directly at what needs to happen. The *real* you must be awakened.

To illustrate this principle further, think again about lasers, light waves that are coherent and "in step." All phases of the laser are moving in the same direction in lockstep at the same time, which is why they can burn through sheets of steel. When your words have coherence and are "in step" like a laser, these words will be filled with the power to change your world.

A Personal "Strong Command" Account

Almost unanimously, people will say the worst thing that can befall a parent is the loss of a child. We saw a friend of ours experience this tragedy. Tim was a single parent trying to do his best to raise his teenage son Kevin, who had asked to live with his father after his parents' divorce. It wasn't easy. Much emotion had factored into the history of pain and bitter fighting before the divorce. The situation was extremely difficult for both father and son. As committed as he was to giving Kevin a happy, well-adjusted life, things were not going as well as Tim had anticipated. Drugs eventually entered into Kevin's life, and his relationship with his father changed dramatically.

Counseling, drug rehab, long father-son weekends, even moving to another part of the city did little to make things better. On a dismal, sleety February evening, Tim came home from work and found Kevin's body. He had overdosed.

> *The shock, the horror, was more than I can put into words even now. I don't think anyone would be helped by*

hearing all that ensued during those next agonizing months, but I guess most of it can be distilled down into two basic questions. "What could I have done to prevent this?" and "How can I ever live with the tormenting guilt I feel?"

Tim, who had discovered the Six Steps on a website we had created, said Step Five was a life preserver. After some sound psychological counseling to help him see he had been a loving and devoted father, and that he had done so much to help Kevin adjust, Tim, on an intellectual level, realized there was probably not a great deal more he could have done to prevent his son's death. Yet on a raw, emotional level, Tim was not able to cope. Some powerful factor had to be introduced to help him.

I really got into that "strong command" step. I had been riddled with grief and guilt, and Step Five seemed made-to-order for me. As many times a day as I could manage, and probably never less than five or six, I would go someplace where no one else was around who could hear me. Of course, in my own home this was no problem, but anywhere else required some creative thinking to find an opportunity. This was not always easy to find because I was loud. I know, you can launch a strong command silently, and it will work, but I chose to do it the loud way. I mean I was fire truck loud!

Hey, here's a good one. I work in New York and at rush hour the noise in the subway stations is so loud, I figured no one would hear me if I bellowed out my command right there in the crowd. As a train roared in, I gave it a go and discovered I was right. No one noticed. Well, you know, even if they did, this was New York, remember, so no one would pay any attention anyway. It struck me so funny that after I yelled out the command, I burst out laughing standing there on the subway platform in a sea of commuters. They didn't pay any attention to all that laughing either!

Tim wants to keep the actual words of his command private because he says it gave him his life back, and he is superstitious about revealing it. It did have to do with calling forth the "real" Tim who had been in a dark cave ever since Kevin's death. It was very short, he says, and involved some unprintable words. But it got results. Whatever it takes—whatever works for you—is right. He did say it took a few weeks before his emotions really heard the command and allowed him to wake up. His son's death has left a lasting scar on Tim's heart, as would be expected. He is doing well, however, feeling less and less guilt and moving on with his life.

A Second Personal "Strong Command" Account

Luisa was coming home after attending a night school class to learn English. Knocked to the ground, raped at gunpoint and brutally beaten, she was left for dead. Eventually she recovered, with few scars other than those on her psyche. The cheerful, friendly young woman of before became saturated with anger and dread. Her attacker has never been found. Luisa sent us the following account and gave permission to share her words as they appear below.

Forgive me, I hope. My English is not good now but soon will be. After I left the hospital I want to do nothing. Only hide. I don't want to go back to work and not want to go back to school to learn English so I could become United States citizen. I don't care about it like before. I was feeling nothing but fear. Always the fear and the anger screaming inside me. Maybe hate is the right word also, no? I had much hate.

Before the Six Steps, maybe it was impossible to get my life back, but now yes, is possible. I did every Lazarus step and now am alive again. I worked hard to come out of my cave. The Luisa cave was very dark. The best step for me is number five because strong command is what works to pull me out of the cave. I hear my voice very loud, very strong. I say it many times every day: Forget that man and how he hurt you, Luisa. Forget. Forget. Come back to life now. I listen and I hear in my heart and now am out of the dark Luisa cave. I think maybe forever.

The English is not so good yet but soon because now I go to my class again. I am a new Luisa. I call myself Luisa Nueva because I have smiles again like before and will be a United States citizen one day.

Luisa finally was able to throw that vicious man out of her world. He had lived rent-free in her mind for too long. He was her constant companion when she was home, at work, and in her bedroom each night as she tried to sleep.

Those who know Luisa see her as a miracle considering the brutal attack she had experienced. The Six Steps had special meaning for her and she was trusting of the process. In addition to her "favorite" Step Five, she especially liked Step Two (Remove the Stone), in which she worked very hard to forgive her attacker. In the words of Shakespeare, "all's well that ends well." Luisa's story has.

Call It Forth Now

You have just read the personal accounts of two people whose lives were filled with tragedy, and who were able to use Step Five to bring their lives back into the "light":

A single-parent father whose son took his own life.

A young woman savagely beaten and raped and left for dead who says Step Five was responsible for pulling her out of "the cave."

Call forth the life in you. The life you want—the one that had been lying dormant and is now being restored to wholeness. Call it out loudly and with absolute conviction and unwavering expectation. Let your words become alive with the creative power within you. Send them out *now*.

Centering Thought for Step Five

Come out! Come out now! I leave the dark cave of the past and I step into the light.

Step Five EXTRA
"A Strong Command"

When you create a strong command, something that will be your constant companion, take your time to come up with just the right phrase. Although you probably won't be yelling it out in the New York subway like Tim, his is an example of just how unique a strong command can be! The strength of your command is your belief and your trust and your commitment to using it as often as possible.

Proclaim It With Passion

If you listen very carefully to your words, you will discover a lot about yourself because your words are actually your distilled thoughts and feelings. When you speak, you send a signal through a neural pathway in the brain. The more you speak the same words, especially if the words are powerful and positive and genuinely felt, the more permanently they instill themselves in your mind.

A short, very pointed, sharply directed strong command *proclaimed with passion* has a powerful impact on your thought patterns, especially when backed by your conviction and emotion. Repeat your strong command often, silently or audibly throughout the day until it becomes so much a part of you that it springs to mind automatically. Being constantly in your mind is exactly where you want it, because that's where it will do its most powerful work.

Whatever Works for You

A few months after attending one of our classes, someone wrote to tell us she uses her command when she jogs. She said she was awkward and ungainly as a child and grew up being told she was clumsy and worthless. In an attempt to reconstruct her self-image, she set a goal of running in the Boston Marathon, which of course entails miles and miles of training just to get into shape for the ordeal. To help break up the boredom and also to help motivate herself, she decided to adopt a phrase meaningful to her. It was a rather short phrase, and in her training she repeats it one syllable per step. "I-am-worth-while, I-am-worth-while, I-am-worth-while ..." She figures that from the time she started her training to the time she finishes the 26-mile marathon, she will have heard herself say the phrase about 100,000 times!

Write It Out

Write out your personal strong command. Look at the words. Feel the emotions and the power within them. If you feel no emotion or there's no power in the words, it isn't the right command. Try again.

Continue to set aside a silent time daily. This keeps you in touch with your inner awareness, providing you with constant guidance in your efforts and adjusting your program as your life improves and transforms.

Step Six
Drop the Old Role

The dead man came out, his hands and feet bound with strips of cloth, and his face wrapped in a cloth. "Unbind him, and let him go."

The impossible has become the possible! What needed to be healed is now healed, and Lazarus has been restored to life. But wait—one final step is missing.

"Final step? What final step? The man who has just emerged from the tomb is alive, isn't he?"

Well ... yes, in a way. Let's take a look. He's still bound from head to feet with strips of cloth, so the process can't be complete. It can't stop *here*. How alive can he be with burial cloth wrapped snugly around his body? No way he can actively live the life he has just been given. What good is a triumph over the impossible if you are still shrouded in the external wrappings of the past?

"Unbind him, and let him go," Jesus now commands. Discard the no longer relevant past. Cast it aside forever, and *be* that person who has just reappeared on the life scene.

Breaking Free

Observe the exact words in the clause *"The* dead *man came out ..."* Would it not have been more accurate to say, "The man who *was* dead came out?" Actually there's another essential point being made here. Obviously, in the story Lazarus is now alive or he could not have walked out of the cave. Yet in a sense he is as good as dead because his hands and feet are still bound with strips of cloth and his face still wrapped in a cloth. What kind of life is that? No, his restoration to life is still not complete.

Jesus didn't give a quick, "Okay, he's out of the cave, so my work is done. I'm outta here." On the contrary, Jesus is eager to complete the final step and immediately demands, *"Unbind him, and let him go."*

This command comes with a price, however. It means baring yourself to life, rid of the former burial cloths with which you had bound yourself. It means listening to and obeying the command you hear within you to break free of the self-imposed wrappings that had held you tightly in the grip of the old imprisoning situation.

We are all guilty, through repeating and repeating certain words and behavior, of "dressing" ourselves in a particular role. This role eventually becomes our identity, and others recognize and support this identity. There we are, wrapping ourselves tightly with the cloth of the past, a cloth that is comfortable. In our own minds, as well as in other people's minds, we become "the victim"—the cancer patient, the lonely widow, the abandoned child, the abused teenager. We think of ourselves as playing that role. Then other people, by their thinking of us and treating us as in that role, are eager to provide us with the winding strips—the burial cloths—which we dutifully wrap tightly around us. So "my arthritis" becomes to a woman's husband a strip of cloth called "my wife's arthritis" and to her children a strip of cloth called "my mother's arthritis" and to those who live next door a strip of cloth called "my neighbor's arthritis" and to her friends a strip of cloth called "my friend's arthritis," and so on. Her identity is so tightly "bound up" with the arthritis that there is no delineation, no place where the arthritis leaves off and she begins.

Unbind her, and let her go.

A Closer Look

Go back now to the opening words of this passage: *"The dead man came out ..."* Does something about that statement strike you? If he were still bound, how did he come out? Obviously he was not bound too tightly to walk. So what's the message here? We can glean from this passage that, yes, you can be "resurrected." Yet if you are wrapped in the same thoughts and mind-set as before, you are the same person as before. You are not fully alive. Your location may have changed, your mate may have changed, or your financial situation may have changed. Unfortunately, your life will not have changed because, with the same approach as before, you will move inexorably toward the same circumstances as before.

"The dead man came out ..." A dynamite lesson is packed into these few words.

"The Crowd Standing Here"

During the final step of the Lazarus event, Jesus utters a very telling statement when he announces, *"I have said this for the sake of the crowd standing here, that they may believe."* A major component of your healing process is getting people to change their perception of you once you have changed. It takes an enormous amount of convincing for someone to see you in a new way. Remember whom Jesus represents in the story. He represents the real you. So it is you who must tell the crowd to see you differently. You tell them by your words and actions.

It's no secret that people resist change, not only in themselves, but in others as well. As a result, when we do successfully achieve a great overcoming, they tend to hold us in the old pattern, see us as the old identity, and try their best to keep us wrapped in those old burial cloths. Do not let them!

A class reunion is a perfect arena for seeing this in action. You could have graduated with someone who is now a world-renowned surgeon, but some of those who knew him in high school as the class clown might say, "Jack, a surgeon? Are you serious? I'd never let him touch *me* with a knife!" To those former classmates, poor Jack is left standing there wrapped in the same old class clown burial cloths.

Lazarus's face was covered by a cloth. His friends could not possibly see him as he was when he was healthy, so their image of him now was as a dead man. When Jesus presents Step Six, he speaks directly to the people gathered there and instructs *them* to take the burial cloths off Lazarus and to see him healthy and alive. Notice that he, himself, doesn't rush over to Lazarus and start ripping off those linen strips. No, because that would not have made the point. The instruction—the lesson—here is that it is up to the family and friends to get rid of what had been holding Lazarus in a non-living role. The family and friends are the ones who have been thinking of him in that role. Jesus admonishes them to think now of Lazarus as restored to life and therefore transformed. *"Unbind him"* ... release him from *your* negative thinking. See him in a new light. *"... and let him go."* Let go of your vision of him. Let go of your thoughts of what he was. Stop thinking of him in the old way.

"Unbind him and let him go."

The Most Important Person in the Crowd

Something is even more fundamental than convincing others: first convincing yourself. The "Jesus" aspect of you—that undeniably faith-filled part of you—must speak to the part of you that doubts: *"I have said this for the sake of the crowd standing here, that they may believe."* Who is the most important person in *"the crowd standing here"*? It's *you*!

You are going to have to make a continual effort to keep the binding strips off in order to convince yourself of your return to life. In time, other people will come to accept the resurrected life you have allowed to come forth, and will treat you accordingly. In the meantime, you will have to hold tightly to your new life. Each day that new life will strengthen and expand until one day you realize the burial strips are completely gone. The "old you" is nowhere to be found.

Step Six of the hidden blueprint in the Lazarus story is "Drop the Old Role," the final step in overcoming the impossible, the final step in healing what needed to be healed.

Old Wrappings and Trappings

What good would the extraordinary return to life have been to Lazarus if he were allowed to remain standing in the garden before an empty cave while still wrapped in yards and yards of linen strips? Would it have been a true return to life if he spent it clad in the trappings of death? Step Six specifically shows that genuine overcoming involves getting rid of the old wrappings and trappings.

To illustrate the point, let's say a child was repeatedly abused sexually by a stepfather. Would she today invite this man to dinner, or ask him to ride with her in her car, or take him shopping with her? She wouldn't even consider it. Yet every time she thinks of him while eating or driving or shopping, every time she allows the thought of him to upset her, or to fan the flame of anger in her, or to rekindle the hatred, shame, and guilt she is still holding onto after all these years, she is inviting him back into her life. Once again he is in charge, commanding her to rewrap herself in those awful burial strips.

Each time she feels those old burial cloths begin to coil around her again, she must make a vigorous effort to shed them. When she can accept her inner resurrection after proceeding through the first five steps of the Lazarus story, she must loosen those cloths and let it all go. Even if she has difficulty forgetting the incidents themselves, she will no longer allow her uncle's past actions to keep her bound in the role of victim. For the first time since that dreadful experience so many years ago, she is free. This release is what will complete her resurrection experience.

That's only an example of how it works. Whatever your own past "identity" was, it is now time to unwrap those strips of cloth and let go of the old role.

Sooner or Later, They Catch on

Once new life is stirring within you—or even just the *expectation* of it has settled upon you—it is essential to take this final step of complete release from the darkness of the past. Throw off the thoughts and feelings of failure. Throw off the fear. They are all "burial cloths" that no longer serve their purpose and must be shed. You can't be fully alive in the present if you insist on continuing to wear the past. Would you put on a brand new outfit and then wear your old clothes over it? Would you drive your car by looking in the rearview mirror?

Your new self is announcing to the world, "I'm different now. Stop seeing me the old way." This announcement comes not via your voice or some celestial trumpet tantara, but via your own actions. You *become* the new identity (you've taken off the wrappings), and sooner or later, everyone will catch on. They catch on because it is genuine. You believe it about yourself and eventually everyone else believes as well.

A Personal "Drop the Old Role" Account

Alcoholics usually find they have to devote extra effort to Step Six. They might be doing well attending Alcoholics Anonymous (AA) meetings and having a sponsor to give them support when they need it, attaining sobriety and starting to put their lives back together. So far, so good, but they are often faced with friends and family who try to hold them in the old role. This happened to David:

I had wrecked my life and damaged my family with my drinking. My boss (who was actually a friend of mine) put up with it as long as he could and finally had to let me go. My children were always tip-toeing around, afraid of upsetting me because then I might scream at them. My wife, poor Julie, took so much emotional and verbal abuse from me, but she never gave up begging me to get help. My friends? Well, they had long ago given up on me.

One alcoholic in a family can affect everyone and everything, and the chaos can become "normal"—a way of life. My family lived like that for years! My children never knew a sober daddy. Our home never knew joy or peace, but it was the day I struck Julie that I knew I had to get help. I was scared to death of what I had become and what I had done to the ones I love. That day was clearly my "wake-up call."

I joined AA, got a sponsor who was always there for me, and I began to reclaim my life. Julie had joined Al-Anon (support for family members), and she and the kids were so proud, so thrilled, when I got my 90-day chip at

AA for my commitment to sobriety. I was in recovery. I was getting better. Over the months, our household changed. No more hidden booze bottles, no more explosive anger on the kids or screaming at them, no more terrible emotional abuse of Julie. I actually got my old job back, and things seemed to be going well. I had it made. Or so I thought.

At first I didn't want to admit it, but there were signs that my family was having trouble accepting the "new" me. They had reacted to my old role for so long that they didn't know how to act with the new one. It seems strange but it's true. They were not able to adjust to what they thought they'd been praying for! They hated the way things used to be, but they had known it so long that our new relationship made them uncomfortable and confused. They were unconsciously trying to put me back into my old role. For example, the kids, with only one functional parent, were used to getting away with things. Now they were being disciplined by another parent—me. Something I should have been doing for years but never did. My wife, who was used to making decisions alone, suddenly was dealing with someone else's input. The family's previous dynamic was being changed, and they were unconsciously fighting it. They were unconsciously trying their best to wrap those horrible old burial cloths around me again. I could hardly believe what was happening. My sponsor often warned me of this common occurrence with recovering alcoholics, yet I never saw it coming.

Step Six was really an eye-opener for me, a life-saver. It made me recognize my situation and gave me an understanding of "the crowd standing there" and what was happening. The good news is that by continually working to "drop the old role," things did begin to shift. I was able to drop the old role and take off those old burial cloths and finally keep them off, which I'll admit was not easy. Through family counseling, AA and Al-Anon meetings, and through patience and love for each other, finally my family and friends learned to unbind me and let me go. Every once in a while, someone may still try to put me back in the old role, but it's not going to happen. I'm going to my AA meetings. I'm keeping in touch with my sponsor. I'm sober. I'm alive now. That's too precious to let anyone take away.

A Second Personal "Drop the Old Role" Account

If you knew Stuart, you would probably agree that he is an extraordinary human being. Kind, warm, of high integrity, devoted to his family, a gifted architect—he's a happy person for whom life has always been easy. The international architectural corporation for whom he worked offered Stuart the opportunity to become project manager for the design and construction of a large industrial complex in Belgium. His wife, Carol, and their two young boys were as excited as he was about the prospect, and almost at once the family began making plans to move. It was early spring, and they could be there in time for the boys to begin the new school term in late summer.

The boys did not make it for the new term. Within three weeks of being offered his new position, Stuart was in the hospital, diagnosed with non-Hodgkin's lymphoma. In his recovery, Stuart stayed at home for seven weeks, committed to rebuilding his health, putting his illness in the past, and resuming his life. During this same period, we (the authors) were finishing this book and Stuart, who happens to be a friend of ours, became curious about the Six Steps. He was so interested, that he made the decision to apply them to his situation.

For Stuart, Step Six was the most difficult and yet the most amazing. How he accomplished it is almost unbelievable:

> *The entire experience progressed from nightmare to dream to just a memory, and sometimes seems it never happened. I vowed I would climb those Six Steps no matter what it took—bad days, better days, not-so-good days, good days. I clung to my commitment to be well and move on with my life. I became a Six Steps fanatic!*
>
> *As weak as I often was, I had no real problem working through the first five steps. They really resonated with me. I know it's an overused expression, but it describes what I felt. Step Six was the puzzler. The idea that I was one of "the crowd standing here" blew me away. Wow! Of course I was one of the crowd, one of the ones who might try to keep me bound in those old strips of cloth and try to hold me in the old role of cancer victim—"poor Stuart, what a shame." Yet I quickly realized I could do something about* me, *couldn't I? I was sure I could discard those rags and leave them behind me forever.*

What about those others in "the crowd standing here"? How were they ever going to let go of "poor Stuart" and accept the new me? By the time I reached that sixth step, I was having more good days than bad and growing impatient to be done with this phase of my life. How do I deal with those others now? Is it even possible? Carol came up with a brilliant plan. Brilliant in theory, but in reality, could she carry it off?

To fill you in on a few facts, when Stuart became ill his company placed the plans for his work in Belgium on hold, hoping he could go ahead with the move in the near future. Because they valued him so greatly, they left it up to him to determine when he felt ready. Meanwhile, their support of Stuart and his family was a major factor in his healing. He was continually strengthened and encouraged by his company's appreciation of him and by knowing the position was his when he was well. At the same time, the success he had with the first five steps was exciting to witness. However, when Carol came up with her plan for Step Six, we have to admit we wondered how it would work.

Stuart: I feel kind of uncomfortable telling this because it may not sound true, but it is true. It happened. I don't know if I'd be here today if it were not for Carol and her daring plan and her relentless effort to make it happen.

Carol: One thing was absolutely clear to me. That "crowd standing here" was going to have to change their ways—immediately. They were going to have to destroy those rotten strips of cloth they'd been holding around

Stuart and see him in a completely new light. No more Poor Stuart, their sick colleague; no more Poor Stuart, their sick friend. Not acceptable. I knew in my heart Stuart could deal with his own perceptions of himself and step into his role, but the eager "crowd standing here" was a different story. They needed something radical to change their perspective, and I was determined to give it my all.

Stuart has always been very popular. So many people genuinely love and care about him. Many prayed and hoped for his recovery. When he became ill, a stampede of well-wishers sprang into action with cards, phone calls and lots of visits. They were concerned about Stuart and meant well. A wonderful thing, right? Now this is where the story gets peculiar.

According to my strategy, all those cards, phone calls and visits were not a good thing. To be frank, all those caring people were keeping the old strips of linen wrapped around my husband. "How are you feeling today, Stu, having much pain?" "I'm praying hard for you to get well, Stuart." "Hey, Stu, think you'll ever be able to take that position in Belgium? We sure hope so. Be a damn shame if you couldn't. We know how much you were looking forward to it." "Take it easy now, dear. You don't want to overdo it and end up back in the hospital." "So how's the radiation treatment coming along, Stuart? Much more to go?" On and on it went, and none of it acknowledging the new Stuart breaking free of all the old stuff and attempting to move on.

I followed my instincts and took it upon myself to become a firewall between Stuart and "the crowd standing here." I explained (with the utmost graciousness, I hope) to each person how they all could really help Stuart by accepting his newfound health and his new life. You phoned to speak to Stuart? You had to promise me you'd stick to the rules before I would give him the phone. You're sending a card or a note? Make it nothing to do with illness or recovery, or I won't let him see it. You rang our doorbell? You only got to see Stuart if you were willing to see him in his new role.

I was brutal! Yet the amazing thing is that after an initial wave of shock, shoulder shrugs and wagging heads and no doubt lots of whispers of disapproval behind closed doors, most of that "crowd standing here" played by the rules. I am convinced that a majority of them began in their own minds to acknowledge Stuart's new role, and were actually able to be authentic with their words. They were catching on.

What a fantastic gift this was for Stuart to be surrounded daily by such positive, uplifting, future-oriented words and visits. Oh, there were some who couldn't do it, sure, but many could. Stuart made such a phenomenal recovery that it surprised even his doctors. I never doubted that Stuart would prevail.

Stuart: I'm trying to be brief with this, which is hard to do because the whole experience was such a life-changing one in so many ways. In spite of people's doubts, and even some opposition, Carol's outrageous (as some described it) plan worked. Aside from writing about it here, the whole experience has been long stored away in the past, and we have moved on. If anyone you know ever needs help with the "crowd standing here," consider trying some variation of Carol's plan. Having a firewall worked for me. Outrageous, outlandish, preposterous? Call it what you wish. I give it a five-star recommendation.

Countless Ways

There are countless ways to utilize the Six Steps of this ancient blueprint. No two people will ever use the steps in the same way. The heartbreaking personal accounts you just read illustrate how two people courageously worked with Step Six to create new lives—not only for themselves, but also for their entire families.

David, an alcoholic, who had ruined his life and had sunk to the lowest ebb.

Stuart, who recovered from non-Hodgkin's lymphoma by working with all of the Steps. However, it was Step Six that worked in a quirky, original way, that delivered the victory.

What great examples they are for all of us.

Do Not Recycle

Regardless of what had been holding you "less than alive," here you are in the final step of your personal "resurrection." Discard the old role with its old wrappings and trappings, and once you discard it, *do not reclaim it. Do not recycle it.* You cannot go forward into the new if you are still clinging to the old. (When a farmer plants seeds, he doesn't keep digging them up to see if they're growing.) Letting go of the old role is the only way you can free up space for the new role to take over. You cannot climb to the top of a ladder while still holding on to the bottom rung.

The part of your life that was in darkness is being healed—is perhaps already healed. Unbind it at last—and let it go.

Centering Thought for Step Six

Spirit of life within me, search my heart and find the wellspring of gratitude there. You have lifted me onto a higher path and given me hope and peace of mind. You are my unfailing strength as I allow the old wrappings and trappings to fall away so I can become the person I was created to be. I am at peace.

Step Six EXTRA
"Drop the Old Role"

We are all guilty, by repeating and repeating certain words and behavior, of "dressing" ourselves in a particular role.

As you worked with Step Six, were you able to identify the "dressing" you had been wearing in your old role? What were some of the words you repeatedly spoke? Do you find yourself still speaking them? What were some actions you repeated and repeated? Do you find yourself still doing them? For some people, these words and actions pop right out, while others may need more introspection. It may jog your memory if you make a list of behaviors you've repeated over and over that you want to change.

Check Out the Crowd

You already know that certain members of "the crowd standing here" will be working hard to push you back into your old role. These are people in your life who can and often do put a negative spin on everything. Even if they may not always be referring to you, their negativity rubs off on all those around them. These are members of the crowd that warn their friend who's decided to get a graduate degree after raising her family, "You can't teach an old dog new tricks." Keep your distance from such people. As you have already read, if you're going to climb a mountain, don't choose climbing partners who are afraid of heights.

If you are buying into someone else's belief about you, carefully check out your own belief about yourself because no one can make you believe anything about you that, at some level, you don't already believe.

Never listen to those who are uncomfortable with the changes you are making in your life. Keep away from those who would like to take your new life from you. These people are not supportive of your goals and your triumphs. They are trying to force you back into your old role and keep you there. They cannot tolerate someone's success. It's called *schadenfreude*, which translates as "finding joy in someone's failure."

You have the power to keep that from happening. Feel *your* power and use it. Believe in your own strength. Let it work for you now.

You are taking on a new life as you let go of the old one. The part of your life that had been in darkness is being healed, perhaps already healed. Allow the old wrappings and trappings to continue falling away, so that you can become the person you were created to be.

Cherish the Gift

Perhaps you originally picked up this book because your life needed a "resurrection." Maybe something within you— some part of you—was waiting to have life breathed back into it. The book is short but the information is complete. In the Lazarus story, every step of the process employed to over- come an impossible situation is here for you to apply to your own situation. The story's hidden blueprint is a gift to you from the distant past. May you cherish the gift and use it well.

Something Invaluable to Keep in Mind

At the beginning of the story, when Jesus was finally ready to go to Lazarus, he said to his disciples, *"let us go to Judea again."* Again! So obviously, this was not his first trip. It implies we can visit a hopeless situation *again*, employ the Six Steps *again*, turn the impossible into the possible *again*, heal what needs to be healed *again*. How comforting to know that if some time in the future you find yourself in another dark cave, you can always *"go to Judea again."* No matter how many times you go to Judea (utilize the Six Steps), the blue- print does not fade, cannot be depleted. Whenever you need it, there it is.

We wish you new peace and healing through the remarkable Six Steps. We trust the clouds of despair and darkness are lifting, and that you have taken this 2,000-year-old blueprint into your heart, where it can do its mighty work.

Call upon the wisdom of the Six Steps in the Lazarus story anytime anything tries to make you feel hopeless and lost. When you do, each new dawn will bring new life for you, and all will be well. All *will* be well.

ENDNOTES

1 **Authors' note:** We have abridged the story of Lazarus here in order to feature passages containing the most meaningful pieces of the hidden blueprint. The complete Lazarus story is in the Gospel of John, Chapter 11 (New Revised Standard Version).

2 Taken from an article entitled "Cure of the Mind," by Maj-Britt Niemi, which appeared in the February 2009 issue of *Scientific American* magazine.

3 Harper & Row, NY, 1950.

ABOUT THE AUTHORS

Mary-Alice and Richard Jafolla have always used holistic teachings and spiritual principles as the core of their professional work. Mary-Alice has been a university instructor with an M.A. in humanities, and Richard has been a substance abuse counselor with an M.S. in counseling psychology. Both were teachers at Life Therapy Institute in Palm Springs, California.

They founded Spirit of Life, Inc., a nonprofit spiritual and educational organization dedicated to all aspects of wellness. In addition, they established and owned health food stores in California, Alabama, Florida and Texas.

While directors of Silent Unity® in the 1990s, Mary-Alice and Richard served as executive editors of *Daily Word*® magazine. They have authored many articles and best-selling books, including *The Quest, Adventures on the Quest, The Simple Truth,* and *Quest for Prayer.* They have appeared on numerous radio and television shows, and have conducted hundreds of lectures, classes and seminars in the United States and England.

From having been contributing editors for *National Greyhound Update* (that's greyhound dogs, not buses!) to maintaining their current websites, *golfnook.com* and *jafolla.com*, writing continues to be a major part of the Jafollas' lives.

B0112